Contents

CW00591692

Introduction

Dear Parents,

Your children have now reached the exciting stage in their lives of attending primary school and their formal education has begun.

You may well be wondering what experiences they are going to meet now that the professionals are helping you to educate them. You may feel that you would like to know more about the actual work your children are engaged in, for example, how reading and mathematics are taught, or what is the purpose of a project. You will certainly want to know how best you can help them along the way.

Education is currently much under discussion and many changes seem about to take place. We are in the process of taking a closer look at what goes on in schools in order to sharpen practice and see where improvements can be made. You, as parents, are involved in all of this because it will affect your children's education, but you may feel somewhat confused by it all. It is important that you have an insight into school life and teaching methods so that you can judge more effectively where change is needed and can appreciate where there is something of great value, which should be kept secure.

The main thrust of the educational reforms are:

1 Freedom of choice of schools for parents.
2 The establishment of a national curriculum, in which the core subjects are the basic skills in the English language, mathematics and science.
3 National tests for children at the ages of 7, 11 and 14, the results of which are to be made public.
4 The possibility of schools 'opting out' of local authority control, with all finances coming direct from central government.
5 More control of finances for Headteachers and school governors and the possibility of a charge for extra-curriculum activities, such as individual music lessons and school outings.
6 More involvement in school decision-making for parents and open information about aims, methods, and children's progress.

Many of the ideas expressed in these reforms are already taking place in schools. For example, most primary schools place their greatest emphasis on the basic skills of language and mathematics, and most test their pupils regularly. Many schools share information about aims and children's progress with parents. The majority of parents get their children successfully into the school of their choice. But it is always salutary to stand back and re-examine the system, to see how standards can be further raised, and how schools lagging behind can be improved. Most people approve of these reforms in prinicple, but there are, nevertheless, some questions which arise.

Will a national curriculum and fixed tests lead to a rigid education and stultify the liberal and imaginative practices now to be found in many primary schools?

Will 'opting out' lead to an undesirable division in the educational system? Will schools no longer under the local authority have access to the in-service training and inspiration provided by the advisory service and Teachers' Centres, now run and funded by local authorities?

Will a completely free choice of school put undue pressure on Heads to admit pupils, thereby creating over-large classes, which would lead to a lowering of standards and a reduction of opportunities for children? What about those parents whose circumstances force them to accept the nearest school? Will it be a free choice only for those parents who have the means and time to implement it?

As you read this book, you will be able to think about these questions, and many more which will occur to you. Listen, too, to discussions about the reforms, and read all you can about them so that, with your increased responsibility and involvement as parents, you can effectively influence your school and make sensible choices when the time comes.

This book seeks to give you a broad picture of primary school life and to provide some idea of what it is reasonable to expect from schools at this stage. Of course, I have written generally, for all schools differ in some respects, but there is an overall pattern which I have tried to show you. The book is a practical one, and provides advice on the various aspects and stages of learning, gives ideas for home back-up and contains suggestions which may help solve the inevitable problems that arise.

In the old days, parents were not encouraged to share in school life and little was explained about it. Parents, understandably, felt left out of the process of education and found it difficult to help and support their children as they wished to do. There was a division between home and school, with the children in the middle. Happily, this situation has changed now, and is continuing to change all the time. Most schools welcome parents and visits are arranged, so that friendly relationships can develop.

Headteachers make a real effort to explain their aims and teaching methods to parents, despite the many claims on their time. Parents can now become school governors, and so bring an influence to bear on their schools, and parents are also encouraged to help in school in many practical ways. All this is to the great advantage of children, teachers and parents.

Do not be afraid that you are going to become a non-person in your children's lives now that they are at school. You, after all, were the first most influential teacher of your children, from the moment they were born, and will continue to be so for a very long time to come. Their whole approach to life is shaped by you – their ability to relate happily to others, their powers of listening and concentrating, their gain in independence and much more. You are also their first teacher in more specific ways; in the development of language, vital in all aspects of learning; in the skilful control of fingers and hands, which leads to the ability to handle tools and perform delicate operations; in the habit of careful observation and keen interest in the world around them. You, in fact, provide the first learning environment. You are more important emotionally to your children than any teacher will ever be – it is your approval they seek, and your interest and time which is vital to them. You alone can give them that feeling of security and self-confidence they need to gain the most from school, with all its challenges.

The more you participate in the process of learning, the more interesting you will find it, and the more your children will benefit from their schooling. The best education stems from a partnership between teachers, children and parents, and where these links are strong, our children, who are the most important, yet the most vulnerable section of the community, can best develop their full potential at school.

Good luck to you all, and may you enjoy these years of your children's education at primary school, as much as I enjoyed my years of teaching.

Margot Chahin

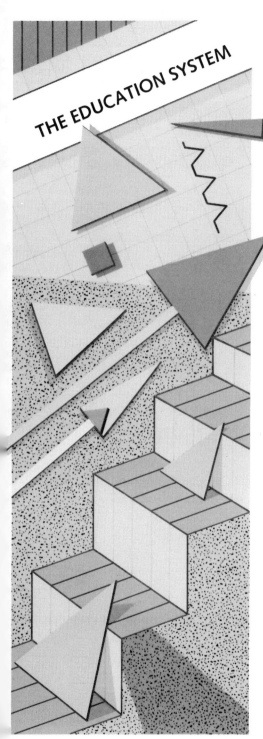

THE EDUCATION SYSTEM

A survey of the system

By law, children must receive full-time education from the beginning of the term after the fifth birthday, either in a school or by some other arrangement considered satisfactory by the Inspectorate. At this point, it is useful to have a look at the education system as a whole and see what is on offer for our children.

The state system

Nursery class or school A nursery school is a separate unit, with its own Headteacher; whilst a nursery class is attached to an infant school. Both take in children from 3–5 years.

Infant schools These are separate units. They have their own Head and specially trained staff for this age-range. Some infant schools will admit children under the age of 5 years, if there are places and if this is the policy of the local authority. They admit children from 5–7 years.

First schools These admit children at the age of 5 or under, but keep them until they are 8 or 9 years old, when they move on to a middle school.

Combined infant and junior school These take children from 5–11 years. The schools are on the same site, but often have a separate building (or part of a building). There is a Junior Head, and a Head of Infants.

Junior schools These take in children between the ages of 7 and 11 years.

Middle schools These take children from the age of 8 or 9 and keep them until 12 or 13 years. They are linked with a first school. Local authorities either run a system of infant and junior schools, or first and middle schools.

Aided schools There are also the religiously controlled state schools, called the 'voluntary sector', known as aided schools. These are schools set up by religious bodies, mainly the Roman Catholic Church, or the Church of England. The state is responsible for the salaries of teachers and for all running costs, while the religious body provides all capital funding, i.e. the building, and controls the governing body and the appointment of staff. Denominational religious instruction is permitted in aided schools. In all other respects, they are similar to other state schools.

Special schools These schools provide education for handicapped children, either physically or mentally, or for children with behavioural problems. Children are sent to special schools if it is believed they cannot benefit from normal state education, or would gain more from a period in a special school. These schools have specially adapted buildings and equipment. Highly-trained specialist staff are employed to work in these schools. The ratio of staff to children is usually higher than in other schools.

The independent sector in education

These schools are not funded by the state, so they charge fees. Most offer scholarships and the government offers assisted places to some schools. Both scholarships and assisted places are decided on a competitive basis. Generally speaking, these schools are more traditional than state schools; but there are some liberal and experimental schools among them. For our age-range, there are:

Pre-preparatory schools These independent schools sometimes admit children at a very young age. Boys are kept until the age of 7 or 8, whilst girls are sometimes kept on until much older. This will probably depend on whether there exists a preparatory school for the girls to move on to.

Preparatory school These schools take children from the age of 7 or 8 years. At the age of 13 the children sit for the Common Entrance examination, which allows them to pass on to a college, main school, or public school. Preparatory schools are very often boarding schools. For further details, see 'Independent Schools Information Service', in the list of addresses, or ask your local authority about the existence of schools in your area.

Who runs state education?

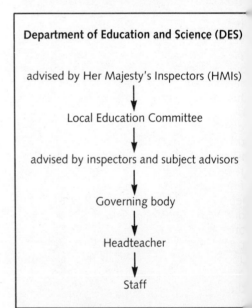

Department of Education and Science (DES)

advised by Her Majesty's Inspectors (HMIs)

↓

Local Education Committee

↓

advised by inspectors and subject advisors

↓

Governing body

↓

Headteacher

↓

Staff

The Department of Education and Science (DES)

This is led by the Secretary of State, aided by his civil servants. It is responsible for:

- the organisation of the whole system, in a general way;
- the supply of teachers and decisions about their salary;
- all building programmes (except in aided schools);
- final arbitration in disputes between parents and local authorities.

The DES is advised and aided by Her Majesty's Inspectors of Schools (HMIs), who keep a watch on what is going on, express opinions and advise. It can make special grants of money available for certain causes, e.g. teachers' courses or special building programmes. (NB Scotland, Wales and Northern Ireland are outside its jurisdiction. They have their own governing bodies: the Scottish Education Department, the Welsh Office and the Department of Education for Northern Ireland.)

The local education authorities

There are 104 of these in England and Wales, 12 in Scotland and 5 in Northern Ireland. They are usually located in the town or county hall, and they each have their own approach and educational policy. The Chief Education Officer leads the Education Committee and broadly determines the educational policy for authority schools. He is aided by a team of inspectors and advisors, who give professional advice on the various aspects of education. The Social Services department works closely with the Education Committee over matters concerning day nurseries, community homes, providing for children in care, giving support to play groups, and so on. As far as parents are concerned, it is the Chief Education Officer and his staff who affect the local schools and make decisions about them.

Who provides the money?

Financial provision is shared between the central and local authorities; the DES gives a rate support grant and the local authority contributes from the rates. In most local authorities, the greater part of the rates is spent on education – about 60% of it. Each school in the authority is provided with an annual sum of money, called the 'capitation allowance'. This is intended to cover running costs, as well as all books and equipment.

The governing body

Each school has its own governing body, and this is made up of:

- nominees of the local authority, usually representing all political parties, and possibly someone from the local community with a particular interest in that school, such as a social worker, or an industrialist;
- the headteacher;
- representatives of the teaching staff;
- parent representatives (soon to be increased).

The local authority has the general supervision of the school, while the Head is responsible for the day-to-day running of it. The governing body comes in between the two. The governors usually meet once a month and receive a report from the Head, which tells of the progress of the school, and informs of any major changes anticipated. It is expected that the governors will take a keen interest in the school, attending functions and supporting the Head. The governors are legally required to hold an open meeting once a year to which parents are invited to attend. Important functions of the governing body are:

- a role in the appointment of staff;
- a general oversight of the schools and its curriculum, with the power to modify if needed;
- discussion of any problems which arise in

the school, such as the suspension of a difficult child or dealing with a question which parents feel has not been satisfactorily settled within the school;
- a role in the use of school finances.

The staffing of the school

The staff of most state primary schools consists of:

Headteacher – to whom all initial queries and problems should be addressed. By law, the Head is responsible for the internal organisation of the school, for the curriculum and how it is taught, and for discipline. Headteachers advise and consult with their staff and usually communicate the school's aims to parents.

Deputy head – stands in for the Head when necessary, has special duties allocated by the Head, and is usually a class-teacher as well.

Teachers – responsible for a class or group of children in the school. They usually remain with their class/group for a complete school year. Some teachers hold posts of special responsibility – for the development of a particular area of the curriculum, e.g. maths, drama or computer studies. In a team-teaching situation, two or more teachers will be responsible for a larger group of children.

Part-time or visiting teachers may work with groups of children for a special purpose or may help to relieve pressure generally.

Secretary – responsible for all clerical work and often familiar with the organisational details of the school.

Ancillary helpers have all-purpose duties; they may comfort the fallen, cope with wet pants, mix the paint, and so on. They sometimes work in the classrooms, under a teacher's guidance.

Catering staff supervise the cooking and serving of school meals.

Dinner-time helpers supervise the children at meal-times and look after them until afternoon school starts again.

Caretaker – responsible for the cleaning, maintenance and security of the building and play areas.

Cleaners – who work before and after school hours.

The prospectus, brochure or information sheet

It is now a statutory duty for each school to provide some kind of information sheet, which will tell you all the details you want to know, such as the roll, number and size of classes, number of staff and specialist teachers. It may say a little about the work and how this is tackled, about after-school activities, the existence of a parent/teacher association, and so on.

It cannot replace the personal visit to the school, when you will be able to meet the Headteacher, see over the school, and assess the general atmosphere. However, is useful since you can browse over it at your leisure.

The school building

It is not wise to judge any school by its building. I have known schools with super buildings to be mediocre, and conversely, ancient schools that manage to create a marvellously imaginative environment. Of course, children (and their teachers) are entitled to a reasonable building, suited to their needs. Such a building makes it much easier to organise the school satisfactorily and enhances the daily life of both children and staff.

The ideal school building is light and bright, in good repair and with plenty of space both in the classrooms and in the hall. There should be an adequate number of toilets and cloakrooms for the number of pupils, provision for sickness and accident, plenty of display boards and storage space. It should also have a good play area outside.

Although the building strongly affects the lives of children and teachers, making their work easy or difficult to carry through, have to say that in the end it is the Head and the staff who make a good school, and not the building. As ever, the quality of education depends on the calibre and devotion of the teachers and other staff in the school.

Parents' right of choice

Can I choose the school my children attend?

Under the 1980 Education Act, parents have the right to 'express a preference' for the school they wish their children to attend. Local authorities must provide a general schools' information' document, which lists the available schools and gives information about schools admission procedures. Although the great majority of children get into the school of their parents' choice, this right to express a preference does not automatically mean that your children will be admitted to the chosen school. The local authority is not at present obliged to comply, though it will try to do so. In the case of an over-subscribed school, the local authority sets priorities for admission. Those children living nearby, within a prescribed catchment area, usually have an automatic right of admission; children with brothers or sisters at the school already; children with medical problems better catered for at one school, rather than another; or, in the voluntary schools, the religious beliefs of the parents all these factors will be taken into account. If your children cannot be

admitted into the school of your choice you have the right to appeal to your local authority for the decision to be changed. This appeal must be put in writing, stating your reasons.

If you live outside the catchment area, getting your children into the school of your choice can be a difficult matter. There should be no problem if the school has places to spare but very often those popular schools with a good reputation are filled to overflowing. If you have a strong preference for any school it is good idea to visit the Headteacher, find out how far the catchment area extends, how long the waiting list is, and so on, before becoming too fixed in your determination.

Can I educate my children at home?

All children between the ages of 5 and 16 years must by law receive 'an efficient education suited to their age, aptitude and ability, either by regular attendance at school, or otherwise' (from the Education Act, 1944). Most people opt for school, but parents are legally entitled to educate their children at home or to make any other arrangements they think fit – providing the children attain a standard of education commensurate with their age, ability and aptitudes. The local authority assesses this by regular visits.

If you are considering doing this, it is right to remember that education is not only a matter of academic progress but also of social and emotional development, and for this children need an outside community. They need the experience of mixing, relating to, and making friends with other adults and children; of sharing, of helping the less able, and of accepting help from the more gifted; of fitting into a routine, learning to lead and to follow, and so on. You also have to think carefully about and provide for physical development and creative work. All of these aspects of education could be catered for at home. Children can be very well taught at home, but they may miss a great deal of fun. There could be some risk of life becoming rather inward-looking for these children.

'Education Otherwise'is an organisation offering support and advice to parents thinking about home-based education. You can find its address on page 94.

Must my children join in religious education?

Religious education is the only subject which by law must be taught in all schools (Education Act, 1944). The Act also states that the school day must include an act of worship. This is loosely interpreted nowadays, and the school assembly may take place at various times, according to the convenience of the individual school. You have the right to withdraw your children from religious education and school assemblies if you hold strong personal beliefs about doctrinal teaching or if you would prefer your children not to receive any instruction in this field at all. Excluding children from anything which regularly takes place at school is sad and can set up unexpected inhibitions later – so very careful thought needs to be given to this decision.

Is school uniform compulsory?

Primary school Heads may not insist on the wearing of a school uniform, though they are allowed to try to promote one. This decision is usually arrived at after discussion with parents. The Headteacher will explain the reasons for wanting to launch a school uniform. It may be for social reasons; or for reasons of cohesion within the school, to help establish a feeling of unity and community; or for reasons of safety, for example, the wearing of suitable shoes and dresses for the activities undertaken; or for a combination of these reasons.

Handicapped children

Handicapped children have a right to an education suited to their needs. Before the Warnock Education Act of 1981, all children with special needs were educated at special schools, with suitably trained staff, special equipment and adapated buildings, small classes, and a high adult:child staffing ratio. The 1981 Act recognised the advisability of integrating children with special educational needs in the general community, as far as possible. suggested that special units should be established alongside the neighbourhood schools. A request for assessment for a chi can either come from the parents or from the local authority. Parents have the right be involved in the decision-making concerning the education and treatment of the child. Parents also have the right to appeal to the Secretary of State of Education, if they do not agree with the local authority's decision about the specia needs of the child.

Health care in school

Medical inspection

When your children have settled comfortably into school life they will be seen by the school doctor. You are encouraged to attend the examination ar often the Headteacher is there too. You w be asked general questions about your children's health. Any worries you may have can be discussed. The school nurse v have previously checked on vision, hearir and dental health; if any treatment is needed, you will be advised where this ca take place. Children with particular handicaps of any kind will be given speci attention. If you are advised to have a defect checked or to follow a certain cou of treatment, you should not feel that thi in any way a criticism of your care at hon Many disabilities are more easily identifie at school, where there is the opportunity constant comparison with other children. This is especially true of emotionally disturbed or persistently backward children.

Your presence at the school medical examination is of great importance because you know your children better than anyone else. You can give the doctor much useful, essential information. Do be absolutely frank when you are discussing past illness and problems; it is your children's welfare under discussion, and they deserve all the resources open to them. Things like bed-wetting, poor appetite, persistent sleeplessness, violent temper-tantrums, refusal to mix with others and so on, can shed light on a problem which could be ended, given the right help.

The school nurse continues to check on vision, hearing, and dental health on a regular basis. When epidemics threaten, e.g. foot infections or hair infestations, the nurse is there to give advice and treatment. Any query which is put forward by a teacher concerning a child can be mentioned to the nurse, who will suggest help and give advice to parents.

Illness in school

For minor accidents like cut knees, grazed hands, etc. all schools are equipped with a first-aid box, which is kept in a safe place and administered by a staff member. A similar box is taken on any school outing. If an accident should happen in school, children are immediately taken to the nearest hospital, and parents are notified. A child who feels unwell rests in a sick-room, or a quiet corner of the Head's room, and parents are contacted. Any practical treatment to relieve the child's condition is given, such as a hotwater bottle, or a warm drink. I have known children wait for a very long time before a parent arrived to take them home. So if you get a call from school, do try to get there quickly; your children really need you (and no-one else) when they are unwell. If your children are prone to attacks of asthma or eczema or anything of this nature, make sure the Headteacher knows, and knows, too, where she can ring for help. Tell her of any measure that can be taken in an emergency.

Glasses, etc.

If your children wear glasses, a hearing aid, a brace, or any other temporary aid, do make sure that the teacher knows if these can ever be removed or should be worn all the time. Children are terribly canny and if they object to wearing the device, will blandly remove it, saying 'I only have to wear it in the mornings'. The teacher needs to be kept in the picture. The same holds for any pills or medicine to be taken during school hours; let the school have it in writing, please!

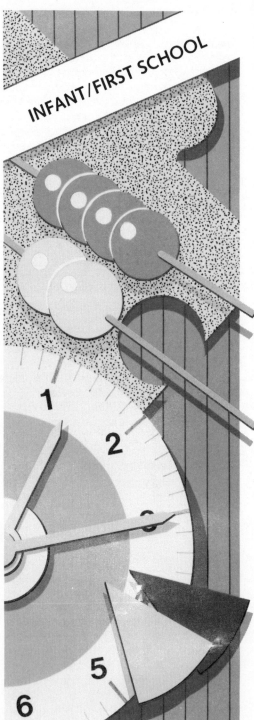

INFANT/FIRST SCHOOL

Choosing a school

Age and time of starting

The first class in the school is usually called the reception class. It is obviously much better for the children if they can spend a full year in this class, building up a stable relationship with one teacher, and working with the same group of children in the same classroom, rather than joining the class half-way through the year, or having to be moved on to allow for the admission of new five year-olds. The age and time of admission will vary from one authority to the next, depending on the policy and number of places available. The Headteachers of the schools you visit will tell you when they are likely to be able to admit your child. If you move house after your children have started school, they can be admitted into another school immediately even in the middle of a term provided you choose one that has sufficient space within the catchment area.

Children remain in the infant school until they have reached the age of seven (or eight in a first school). The change to junior/middle school is always made at the beginning of a school year i.e. in September.

How to set about choosing

Although by law you have the right to state a preference for a school, in practice most parents choose a neighbourhood school. This seems sensible as the children will be able to form friendships with nearby families, and a long journey is avoided. If you live in a large town there may be a choice of two or three schools nearby, and you will want to visit all of them so that you can compare them. If you live in the countryside, your children may have to travel to a nearby village or town for school in which case transport is usually provided by the local authority. Remember that you can choose to place your child at any primary school, providing there is room and you can guarantee regular and punctual attendance. In some instances, parents feel so strongly about a particular school that they are prepared to make great efforts to enable their children to attend it.

Well before your child's fifth birthday, pay a visit to your local education authority to obtain information about all the schools in your area. You will be advised:

- which schools are heavily over-subscribed;
- if there is a catchment area in operation for any school;
  about aided schools, and which religious denomination supports these.

If you are interested, they will give you information about independent schools, too. They may be able to provide you with school brochures. Armed with this information, discuss the possibilities at home, and decide which schools you would like to visit.

The next step is to make appointments with the Headteachers. Try to see as many schools as you can, even if you already have a pretty firm idea which one you are going to choose. The more you see, the more the idea of what you want in a school of your choice will become clarified. After all, it may be quite a long time since you set foot inside a school for little children, and things have changed considerably – so have a good look.

Visiting schools

It is not advisable to take your children with you on a first visit. This is your visit, designed to give you the chance to talk, discuss, ask questions and to see over the school. Once you have decided on a school, that is the time to arrange visits for the children.

First of all, you will meet the Headteacher and he/she will tell you about the school and answer your questions. (Please remember that Headteachers are busy people often involved with teaching the children so, although you will be warmly welcomed, there may not be unlimited time to spare). Think out your questions beforehand and make a note of the answers, so that you can keep things clear in your mind; it can be bewildering when so much information is given out at once.

Some questions to ask

These are some sensible questions that Heads are frequently asked:

1 What is the enrolment procedure? What is the length of the waiting list? What is the age at which children can be admitted? What are the class-sizes and the school roll?
2 How many staff are there? Are there any specialists?
3 Is there a parent/teacher association, or similar body? How many parent-governors are there? Can parents help in school? Are there school functions and social events?
4 Are teaching methods traditional or more progressive? Is there any homework? Are the children tested or screened? Is extra help given to children with learning difficulties? Are bright children allowed to forge ahead? Are individual records kept, and can we see them?
5 How are we kept in touch with our children's progress? Are there open days, end-of-term reports, progress reports, etc.?
6 What are the school rules, discipline and rewards?
7 Does creative work, such as art, craft, music and drama take place, and what are the facilities? What kind of physical education is provided? Do the children go swimming?
8 How is religious education taught? (If

13

you cannot go along with the practice in the school, it is sensible not to choose that particular one.)

9 Is there a set uniform – complete or partial, and is there a used clothing system? Are special clothes and equipment needed for games or PE?

10 What are the arrangements for school meals? Are packed lunches permitted?

11 What happens in cases of illness or accident?

12 Are children supervised at play-times, lunch-breaks and before and after school?

13 Which school do the children move on to? Are there links between the school and neighbouring junior schools?

You will not, of course, want to ask all these questions. Some of them may well wait until you have decided on the school. But by asking some of them you will be able to build up a picture of the aims and life of the school and you will be giving the Headteacher the opportunity to talk about the school.

Taking a look around

During the tour of the school, when you go into the classrooms, do not expect a long conversation with the class-teacher who will be much too busy with the children. Your guide will be able to explain what is going on. You may get the chance to talk to the children themselves.

On your way round the school there will be much to look at, and it may help you to focus on one or two particular points:

1 Is your welcome a warm one, with smiles from the adults and children? Are the children confident and ready to talk? Does the Headteacher appear to have good relationships with the staff and children?

2 Do the children appear to be happy and well settled into their activities? Is the atmosphere calm and ordered, without seeming repressive?

3 Are there plenty of books around the school, in good condition? Is there a computer?

4 Is there evidence of exciting displays o' work, in addition to paintings?

5 Is the building sensibly planned for sm. children, with adequate cloakroom anc toilet facilities? Is there adequate outsi playing space?

6 Are there plenty of learning aids: a number line, a number square, a calendar, lists of useful words, and so on?

If you are able to visit several schools you will learn to distinguish between the scho which gives a happy and lively impressio but shows little evidence of work and the school where real learning is taking place Look for evidence of mathematics; writte work, however simple; signs of a purposeful project.

Once your decision is made, give the school your full backing because your support will make all the difference to th Headteacher and staff and, ultimately, tc your children's education. You are bounc have the occasional upset – after all, this happens even in the best of families – an this occurs, ask for an appointment with Head to talk it out. With the Headteache inside knowledge of the school, he/she i the best position to explain things to yo and to effect any changes which are needed to put matters right.

Registration

Once you have decided on your school, another appointment should be made w the Headteacher, for official registration the school roll. At this stage, the Headteacher will need to ask you some questions, too. These are designed to gi the information required to complete obligatory records for the local educatio authority. More importantly, the answer provide a background knowledge of you children, so that the teaching staff can help them to the best of their abilities. These questions will be sympathetically asked so you should not feel that the Head is 'probing' into your private life. The information will be kept confidential.

The Head will need to know:

- the date and place of birth of your children, and will probably ask to see the birth certificate;
- about the health and development of your children. Be absolutely frank about this. If there have been problems, such as a late start to walking or talking or periods of severe temper-tantrums, tell the Headteacher all about this as the knowledge will enable the staff to help your children more fully;
- your home address and telephone number; and, if you are working, similar details of your place of work. You may be asked what work you and your husband do;
- if you are a one-parent family (Mum or Dad), or have been separated or divorced, or have re-married, or are living with someone as a permanent partner. Don't mind telling these things; the Headteacher needs to know in order to avoid embarrassment or hurt to your children.

The Headteacher may also ask:

- whether your children attended nursery or playgroup and if so, which one. Whether they enjoyed it or whether there were any particular problems. If they have never been to any pre-school unit the Headteacher may ask if they are used to leaving you;
- questions about diet, since it is likely that the children will join in school meals. It is a good idea to tell the Head about any peculiarities in connection with meal-times; for example, that they eat very little, or are slow eaters, or cannot manage a knife, and so on. This information will help the staff to deal with your children sympathetically at meal-times;

- questions about health; the name of the family doctor, whether your pregnancy and consequent birth were normal, whether your child has ever been in hospital.

You may be informed about the way religious education is introduced in the school. If you hold any special doctrinal beliefs, this is the time to tell the Head.

Once the official business is over, you will be invited to see round the school again, perhaps with a special introduction to your child's future class-teacher. Ask about ways you can help prepare the children for school. You may be loaned some books or games to play with them. The Head may recommend some books for you to read.

Admission

You will be anxious to know when your children will actually start school and how they will be admitted at the beginning of their first term. Most Heads are fairly flexible about this, finding the best solution for their particular school. In a large or very popular school there may be as many as 30 or more children starting school in the same term; in this case, the way they are admitted needs careful thought.

There are several ways of doing this:

- the traditional way of admitting all new-comers on the first day of term;
- to stagger the arrival of the children, thereby giving the teacher and children a better opportunity to get to know each other. The children are admitted a few at a time; say, six on the first day, another six two days later, and so on, until the class is complete. By the time the last batch have arrived, the first-comers are old hands and can help the latest arrivals find their way about;
- to admit half the children for mornings only and the rest for the afternoons only, until they have become familiar with the

teacher and are used to the idea of school.

There are probably many more variations, each designed to help the new entrants to settle into school happily without great emotional upsets. Some parents fear that missing time in school at the beginning may hold back their children's progress. Don't worry about this. The first week or two in school is always used for settling in; work will not be affected at all.

And now to school

The very first day

This is certain to be an exciting and slightly tense day for the children (and for you!) so try to approach the great day quietly and casually so that the tension does not mount up too much. Have all the treasures packed in the school bag and the clothes sorted out ready to avoid rush in the morning. Get up in good time (the children will probably be hopping around in great spirits, from an early hour!) and give the usual breakfast. Any departure from normal procedures should be avoided.

If possible, link up with a friend on the way to school. Most schools welcome parents into the cloakroom at first. You will be able to see that they find their peg, help them with their clothes and shoes, and then show them cheerfully but firmly into the classroom where the teacher and their friends will be awaiting them with lots of lovely things set out to do. Say goodbye casually, making absolutely sure that they know you will be returning to collect them at home-time.

It is not sensible to prolong your stay in the cloakroom, nor to continue to provide this support for too long. The cloakroom is not usually a very large area and it can become very crowded and confusing for the children. As soon as the children have settled into the new venture and know their

way around, that is the time for you to bid bright farewell at the school door, and soon, at the school gate. You will be proud of the independence your children have gained as you watch them running happily into school with their friends.

What about those who cry?

However well-prepared the children are for school you can never tell how they are going to take it until the day for starting actually arrives. Most settle in with the minimum of fuss; but there are always one or two who cry and cling distressingly when the moment of parting comes. This is understandable. Teachers are prepared for it, so if this happens with your child, don't feel embarrassed or let down. After spending some time in the classroom, doing your best to calm them and link them to a friend, the best thing to do is to hand them over to the teacher or helper, screams and all, and leave them to deal with it. Your difficult job at this point is to GO, even though you will doubtless feel very upset. Don't linger around, as this only prolongs the agony for both of you. Most children stop crying once you are out of sight. Heads are most sympathetic to parents in this distressing situation and will not mind at all if you phone sometime during the morning to find out if all is well. It is far better to do this than to sit at home imagining your children weeping inconsolably at school, when all the time they are playing blissfully at the sand-tray! Some children – a very few – take a long time to settle into school and parents come to dread the daily crying scene in the cloakroom. It is worthwhile considering if a more flexible arrangement would help for a while, say, part-time schooling or a shorter school day. In some cases it may be the wrong moment to start school; perhaps there is a new baby, or an upsetting disturbance in the family. Discuss this with the Head, who may already have her own ideas about a solution.

Meeting the children at home-time

It is very important that you meet your children from school on time, especially for the first few days – any delay feels like an abandonment. If you are unavoidably delayed, phone the school so that the message can be passed on to prevent the children from worrying. Alternatively, ask a relative or neighbour to meet the children for you – and here again, a phone call or verbal message is necessary, since no teacher will hand over a child to a stranger. Most schools make arrangements for children awaiting their parent, perhaps in the playground if it is fine, with a supervisor, or altogether in the hall, to listen to a story. Where there are many working parents, some inner-city schools organise tea and play-activities until their parents can come to fetch them. In some areas there are special centres for this.

The first month/term

When children first start school, and for a long time to come, they become very tired. The reasons for this are manifold and various: the school day is longer than the nursery or playgroup; the community in which they pass the day is much larger and noisier; the routine makes more demands upon them; the discipline is more evident and the playground has to be dealt with. We could continue this list for a long time but the upshot is that the children feel exhausted at the end of the day. They need to come home to a familiar atmosphere which does not make new demands on them and where the environment is calm and quiet. Above all they need some individual time with Mum and Dad. So do not plan any activities for the evenings and try to keep all special happenings for the weekends when they will be really enjoyed as something different from school. The children will want plenty of sleep. Early nights are a good idea, but they will also need time to play, watch their favourite television programme, look at a story book with you, and so on.

School meals

When your children attend school full-time, they will probably have their mid-day meal at school. Although this is best avoided at first, the demands of distance and work usually offer no option. The social pleasure of eating with friends, and sometimes teachers, is an important aspect of the meal and school dinners quickly become an eagerly anticipated part of the day. Make sure your children have had the experience of eating a meal without your supportive presence, and that they can conform to normal meal-time behaviour. It is worth noting that children are not forced to eat food they really dislike nowadays, though they are encouraged to try 'a teeny bit' of everything. Food fads often disappear after a few weeks of school meals. They are usually served on a cafeteria basis and often offer a choice to children. They are supervised by a staff member (often the Head) helped by ancillary staff. Children are often allowed to take packed lunches to school, but no primary child is usually given permission to buy food outside. Special catering arrangements can be made for Jewish or Muslim children and for those with special complaints which affect their diet. Local Authorities are not obliged by law to provide school meals but most do. The charge for meals varies with the authority, and is usually reasonable.

Children's worries

In spite of the children's delight in school, some problems may arise from time to time, especially at first while they are adjusting to the school community. Some common problems are:

School meals are a pleasurable social occasion.

Exhaustion, emotional tension and over-excitement These can lead to crotchety behaviour, temper-tantrums and possibly a regression to babyish habits – baby-talk, thumb-sucking, bed-wetting, and so on. Or the children may become very clinging, and refuse to leave you. The first thing to do is to let the teacher know about these signs of stress so that she/he can watch out for difficult moments of the day and give extra support.

Be patient and give the child plenty of extra love and attention at home. Things will probably settle down when they have become more accustomed to the demands of school life. If the stress symptons persist, go and have a further talk with the Head and class-teacher, and try to think of anything which may have upset the child. Between you all, you will be able to give the extra attention and support needed at this time.

Playtime A fear of the playground can cause distress. This can seem alarming to small children and at first some aspects of playtime can give rise to apprehension: the noisy milling crowds of children, most of them unknown; the 'rough' boys, (and probably girls, too); the absence of the class-teacher; the worry about finding the way back to the classroom or to the toilet. Most schools organise things so that new entrants are introduced to the playground gradually. They may have their playtime at a different time from the rest of the school or older children may be asked to look after them or their own class-teacher may join them outside for a week or two. Rest assured that all the staff and the older children will be aware of this problem and will do their best to make the little newcomers feel at home.

I haven't any friends! Some children find difficult to relate to others. They become very distressed as the days pass by and it appears they have no special friend. This is not likely to arise until after a few weeks at school but it can be a real problem, causing

Starting School

When I started school I was very excited before I went in but when I got in I hated it because there were alot of big people there and then I was very nervous but when I got in to class I found out that we hardly did any work. The first thing I did was painting and I drew a house that was not very good. Then it was play time and that was not very bad because I had some crisps. When I came in everyone had some milk but me because I did not like it and then I went home and then I found out that it was called Chard School. My teacher was called Mrs Jenkins and she was about forty years old. Luckily James and Richard were there to look after me.

Peter 7.9yrs

them to become unhappy at school. There may be several reasons for this:

- very shy or inward-looking children may not be able to make the necessary overtures to others, nor respond to their friendly approaches;
- bouncy, over-confident and even aggressive children may want to dominate the scene too much, and so put the other children off;
- the problem may not exist at all in reality, being a figment of the imagination in the mind of the over-sensitive child.

This problem is not likely to arise if you have been able to link up with another child before your children ever entered school. If you were unable to do this, do start now. Find a child who lives near and join forces for the journey to school and help establish a relationship. If this fails, talk to the class-teacher who may be able to tell you what the trouble is and make plans at school to help the children concerned.

School is forever! Some children start school with confidence only to become difficult after a few weeks, much to the disappointment of their parents who thought they had got it absolutely right! It is usually because children have realised that this process of dashing off to school every morning, rain or shine, is a permanent fixture and will go on **FOR EVER!** Their carefree days are apparently gone for ever and the prospect exhausts and daunts them. This is when they begin to show signs of stress, and develop a dislike for going to school.

This period does not usually last for long and you will have to be strong-minded and keep them going. Make sure that they are getting plenty of rest and sleep, because it is tiredness which often causes this mood. To help them overcome their antipathy to school, break up the week into psychological periods. Find or invent something to anticipate; on Monday look forward to a special television programme; on Tuesday, plan a favourite tea and a story; on Wednesday invite Granny to tea, and then talk about the weekend, which could include a special outing. This will carry the children through the week and help them to realise that there are breaks in the weekly routine of school.

Holidays can also be discussed and plans made. It is a question of helping your children to accept the pattern of school, weekends, school, leading to holidays.

The really important thing to remember is that all problems and difficulties are best discussed with the Head and/or the class-teacher. You should feel that you can talk about any aspect of school life that bothers you, and that you can approach the teacher in times of need, rather than worrying by yourself at home. They will probably be meeting the same problem at school, so it is sensible to share your ideas and help each other to find a solution. Small day-to-day problems, or ones that concern classroom life, are best taken to the class-teacher; while more serious and far-reaching ones should be discussed with the Head, who will always include the class-teacher in seeking a solution. You will soon learn to trust the staff, with their experience and expertise. You will realise that, like you, they have the happiness and progress of your children at heart.

Inside the school

When setting up the classroom the teacher aims to create an environment where the children will be happy and where real learning can take place. You will notice that the tables are arranged in small groups. All the equipment is carefully stored, so that the children can get at it AND replace it easily. The walls are bright with teaching aids, labelled paintings and stimulating information, and there is space for the children to work on the floor. There will probably be a carpet area where the books provided can be quietly enjoyed. It is, in fact, a room specially designed for children.

You will notice that the children are engaged in many aspects of learning, and the atmosphere is relaxed, yet purposeful. There will be some movement and chatter, as the children fetch the materials they need or discuss their work. The teacher will be circulating, helping first one group, then another; and all the while her experienced eye will check over the activities of the whole class. She is likely to be sitting at her desk only occasionally. At first sight, this scene may appear a complete confusion to you. As you look closer, you will begin to see the structure more clearly, and will notice how skilfully the teacher manages to keep everything going according to her plan.

Organising the day

The teacher will try to plan the daily routine so that:

- she can fit in with the rest of the school, over matters such as assemblies, PE, TV sessions, and so on;
- the daily pattern is as regular as possible

A corner of the classroom. Here you see the informal grouping of the tables, and the well mounted display on the walls. Notice the concentration with which the children are working.

to provide a stable framework for the children;

- every child has an experience of reading, writing and number work daily;
- each child works in varied ways (as a class-member, in a group, as an individual) and engages in practical work as well as more formal work in books;
- each child has the opportunity for a free choice of activity each day, and that, over a period of time, engages in all the choices available.

In doing this, the teacher must keep track of each child's progress, keep records of the work, and every day she must set and maintain the right atmosphere for learning.

Not an easy task, you will agree, but one which most teachers take in their stride.

When are they taught as a class?

On the many occasions when the children are taught as a class, the disparate group of children are welded together to form a viable teaching group. These times are likely to be:

- all occasions when a special area, particular equipment, or a specialist teacher is involved – such as PE, music, drama, TV sessions, playground games and similar activities;
- all general teaching or discussion sessions where the information is useful for

everyone, such as talking about a project, practising counting, learning the days of the week, and so on. Much teaching in the basic skills takes place at these times;
- for personal news, when the children take the floor;
- for all stories, poems, rhymes etc;
- for religious education;
- sometimes for practice in handwriting, especially as the children move up the school.

There are also the occasions when the class joins in with the whole school: for some assemblies, for a special visit from outside, for a celebration such as a party, or for a talk from the Headteacher, and similar events. Children usually enjoy these times, and through joining in, begin to feel a part of the school and a member of a larger community.

When are they taught in groups, and why?

Most teachers organise their class into groups so that:

- the children's different speeds of learning can be catered for more easily;
- the teacher can interact and discuss with each group in turn, and in this way make economical use of her time;
- it is easier to organise the day's activities;
- the equipment can be shared and enjoyed by all the children in turn;
- a greater variety of activities can be offered because the groups are small – for example, it is practical to set up a table for junk modelling for one group only, whereas to do this for a great number of children would daunt any teacher;
- a less rigid organisation is created for the children and they learn in a more natural way, suited to their young age;
- there is opportunity for plenty of social exchange, too.

Children are likely to be working in groups when:

- they are practising the basic skills of reading, writing stories or news, and working at number/maths. The groups, in this case, are usually decided by the stage the children have reached. This makes sense for discussion. Of course, each child will be doing his or her own work, either in a book, or through a 'game' or whatever, but the stage of the work and its focus will be the same for the whole group;
- they are engaged in demanding activities, where the numbers must obviously be limited, such as sand and water work, woodwork, craftwork, dressing up and domestic play;
- they are working at the project or any special centre of interest which the teacher has launched.

When do they work by themselves?

Children need times during the day when they can withdraw from the mass and follow their own choice of activity. These are important times for all children, but especially for the introverted, disturbed or exhausted child. Children need the experience of choosing, selecting the right material for the job, settling down with concentration and sticking to the task in hand.

Any classroom activity can be followed through individually, and you would be surprised to see how many children actually choose to do a piece of maths or writing, if offered a choice. Of course, lots of them choose the more obvious 'toys' as a relaxation: things such as the farm set, the bricks, or the puzzles; others prefer crayoning, painting, cutting and glueing; whilst others love to look at a book. All the same they are learning through their play.

Play in the classroom

Sometimes parents become concerned that

their children appear to spend part of each day in playing. Play, they think, should be left behind when they start school. But what is 'play'? It has been described as a spontaneous activity chosen by the child and carried out for its own sake. This activity is followed through with intense concentration because the motivation is so great.

Before they ever start school our children have learnt an enormous amount – about the world around them and about themselves and what they can do. They have amassed the words to describe what they are doing. They learnt this mostly through play, which is the natural method by which young children learn. It is a great mistake to think that play is unimportant, or to take it lightly, thinking of it merely as a means of recreation. When children start school they still need the stimulus of play, in order to learn. Those who become deeply involved in 'play' are able to become equally involved in 'work'. Much that starts as play evolves into work, and this is especially true at school, where the teacher is on the look-out for such useful starters. Play is directly linked to intellectual development and this is why it has its place in school.

As the children move on up the school, some of the play activities will be gradually phased out as the need for them diminishes; other things, such as drama, music-making, and creative work in art and craft take their place.

Planning the work of the school

This is done by the Headteacher, together with the school staff. Meetings are held to work out a strategy and structure in each area of the curriculum and the work is carefully planned so that no stages are omitted. The necessary books and equipment are chosen. Work standards are discussed and styles of handwriting, methods in maths teaching, individual and class records, provision for slow and very quick learners – all come under survey.

The teaching in schools is not a haphazard process, but is carefully planned. These plans are under constant discussion and revision. The Head has the overall responsibility but most Heads are pleased to consider the ideas of their staff when finalising decisions. After all, it is the staff who have to carry out the day-to-day implementation of these plans.

The role of the teacher

The class teacher quickly becomes a very important person in your child's life. I am sure you will hear a great deal about this teacher. 'My teacher says . . . ' grows to be a perpetual refrain in the home! The teacher needs a rewarding relationship with the children since the youngsters cannot learn satisfactorily unless they feel secure and happy. In the first few years of school life, the class-teacher is responsible for teaching everything and remains with the children all day. This is an advantage to them, since they gain emotional stability from being with the same adult, in the home-base of the classroom, where they spend most of the day.

The teacher is responsible for:

- setting up and maintaining the apparatus and the classroom;
- preparing work;
- assessing work, planning individual programmes of work for children and keeping records;
- the development of the children into well-adjusted members of the community.

Supporting your children at home

Praise any work brought home, because everything has taken time and effort, even the most incomprehensible-looking things! Mount the painting on your kitchen wall;

23

listen to the children reading the book; discuss the ingenuity of the model. I am sure you will do this instinctively because you will feel so pleased with the work and these treasured offerings are touching. Parents who give the work a passing glance or casual comment, devalue it for the children.

Homework

It is not generally the custom to set homework in the infant/first school, but your children might come home with a few words or number facts to learn. They may be given a few spellings to check over or, as they reach the top of the school, a story to finish, or a book to read. This will not be on a regular basis, but as the need arises. Most children do not mind doing this, in fact, some feel very 'grown-up' with homework – just like their older brother or sister.

Give them your support in this, especially with any learning work, because young children cannot manage this by themselves, they do not have the techniques. See that they have a quiet place to work and find the time to help them. Make a game of it: 'Every time you get it right, you get a counter, and if you get it wrong, I'll have a counter.' This sort of approach makes it fun.

Finding things out

Children are quite often asked by their teachers to see what they can find out about interests which arise in school, especially those from the class project. Young children cannot do this for themselves. You are in the perfect position to help them. There is nothing more likely to stimulate their interest in the work at school than this joint effort at home.

Talk, talk, talk!

Lively discussion, 'straight' conversations, questions and answers over a wide range of subjects, are possibly the surest way of helping your children to get the most from school work. Through discussion they learn:

- how to listen;
- how to use words and sentences;
- new and interesting vocabulary;
- how to sustain and extend an interest;
- how to ask sensible questions;
- how to think about their answers;
- many new facts about their environment.

Personality clashes

"I don't like my new teacher"

Problems sometimes occur when the children move on to a new class in school. They tend to dislike changes of class-teacher and room. They resent this new adult, and will not even try to relate to him or her. Give this situation time and it will settle down, as the children become adjusted to the new set-up. Get to know the teacher yourself and talk about him or her with the children. Their loyalties will soon be transferred to the new teacher and all will be well.

"They don't seem to be getting on in this class"

This complaint is sometimes heard from parents who, like the children, have gained confidence in the former teacher, and find it difficult to assess what is going on in the new class. Again, you must give the situation time before you begin to judge it. The teacher may have a new approach to the work, necessary at this stage. The work may be more demanding, requiring more effort, which the children are reluctant to give. The apparent lack of success is closely linked with the children's attitudes. Ask the teacher about the direction the work is taking, so that you are in the picture. At the same time, check up on your child's classroom behaviour. Learning is a two-way process with the teacher and children working together to achieve success. If your children are uncooperative and disruptive – or just lazy – they will not progress. They may resent any disciplinary action the new teacher is obliged to take, such as seating them at a separate table, or insisting that the work is finished at playtime.

If your child is behaving badly, please try to back up the teacher. Neither your child, nor the others in the class can learn properly, if the discipline is bad. Let your child clearly understand that you are upset by this and that it is not to continue. Then make a point of checking up with the teacher, to see that it has stopped. You and the teacher together will certainly come out on top!

In the final event, if things do not settle down and you are still concerned about your child's unhappiness or lack of progress, make an appointment with the Headteacher, giving the reason for your request so that he or she can do some 'homework' first: looking at the books, observing school and classroom behaviour, noticing relationships, and finding the views of other staff, especially the former class-teacher. The Head will be in the best position to find a solution.

Discipline

This is a thorny question for many parents. You will have your own ideas and standards. Most of us agree that children do need some kind of discipline, just as we know that praise and rewards are necessary. Children need a secure framework in which to carry out their lives; they need to know what is acceptable behaviour, and what is beyond the limit. So discipline is necessary, but what kind, how much and when? Whatever you decide on, make sure that your rules are consistent and do not vary from day to day, according to your mood. Nothing is more worrying for children than to try to conform to rules which do not always apply; they will probably end up by ignoring the lot.

School discipline

Discipline is essential in schools for three main reasons:

- for the physical safety of children in all circumstances;
- for establishing a proper atmosphere where learning can take place;
- to ensure the happiness and emotional security of the children and to encourage good relationships throughout.

The rules and behavioural expectations of the school are likely to be explained and discussed with the children, most of whom will accept the necessity for them. These rules will sometimes insist upon an immediate response to commands, for example, in the playground, in the swimming pool, or whilst doing PE – 'STOP' at the signal. We live in difficult and often dangerous times and teachers in school, responsible as they are for your children, must be able to receive an instant response from them. The rules will also insist that children behave suitably around the school and in the classroom, so that work can progress. They will try to ensure that children behave responsibly to each other and to all adults in the school, namely, no bullying, no rudeness to the 'dinner ladies', no maltreatment to the building or equipment.

The rules are likely to be few and simple, but rigorously enforced. Children are uncannily good at knowing when you don't really mean what you say and will quickly come to ignore all restraints if these are not held to firmly and consistently.

Find out exactly what is expected of your children at school and what, if anything, is banned. Talk about the school rules and codes of behaviour with them and then back the school up.

Rewards and punishments

The greatest reward for children in school for good work or good behaviour, is the praise and pleasure of their teachers and class-mates. This might take the form of a mention in assembly, some work on public display or an admiring comment by a friend. Even more, your delight in their achievements is the greatest incentive for further efforts. 'What a beautiful piece of writing!' or 'I feel really proud of you for sticking up for Tommy in the playground!' Comments such as these are the best rewards children can have. Sometimes in schools there is a system of visible rewards for work well done, such as a sticker or star in the book, or a table for the display of extra-special work. Or there may be a badge for children who have tried particularly hard to be polite or kind or to control a temper. These small encouragements are a form of public recognition for effort, which we all need.

Punishment for bad behaviour is usually in the form of withholding a privilege or removal from the activity in question or from the classroom. For example, children who continually misbehave in PE may be sent back to the classroom to work with a helper; children who keep on scribbling on the books of others will have to rub it out and may be placed by themselves to work; children who are over-aggressive in the playground will not be allowed out. Along with this practical action, the teacher will talk about the incident with the child and hope to show why such behaviour is unacceptable in school.

Children are not usually punished for poor work, unless this is done deliberately; in which case they might be required to do it again, or finish work off at playtime. Unsatisfactory work is rarely intentional; what is needed is extra help to boost confidence and to overcome the problem. You will probably be called in to help and your cooperation at home with a little extra work will usually do the trick.

If your children do persistently behave badly at school (everyone has their off-days!), the Head is likely to invite you to discuss this. You can help by telling the Head if the children have been behaving in a similar way at home or if some aspect of school life is upsetting them. If your children come home with hair-raising stories of what teacher has done to them at school, do check up on this before you charge down to the school. Outraged children can exaggerate. It is natural for us to bridle if we feel our children threatened in any way but try to keep cool. Remember that there must be a reason for the punishment, whatever it is. The teacher will always explain the circumstances to you, and your best reaction is to say something like this: 'Well, if you really pushed Mary off the ropes, I'm not surprised the teacher sent you out of PE – I would have done the same!' In the rare event that you feel a real injustice has occurred, talk this out with the Headteacher. Leave the Head to deal with it, and try to forget about it. It does no good harbouring resentment, rather look ahead to better things.

How to help your children accept school discipline

Children who have not met a reasonable discipline at home, are likely to find it hard to conform to the expected standards at school. So you can help your children by setting your own expectations at home and by reinforcing the school discipline. After all, school rules are mostly commonsense ones, and useful everywhere.

Can they sit still and listen for short periods?
Can they follow instructions?
They should not shout all the time!
Can they share toys?

Working with children, I have found:

- children will accept rules of discipline if the reasons for these are explained;

- children have a strong sense of fair play and it is wise and right to go along with this. For example, if you let your elder child choose the story one night, promising the younger one the same privilege tomorrow, then carry this out otherwise next time your decision will not be accepted;
- you should ALWAYS do what you state you are going to do. Don't promise treats, or concessions if there is doubt about carrying them out. NEVER threaten punishment you have no intention of following through.

Try to avoid 'nagging' the children and sounding 'cross' when you are correcting them. Sometimes the more distraught you become, the worse your children will behave, and a real battle will develop.

Discipline rules need to be discussed with all the family. Mums, Dads, and Grans must all be in it together, or you will find one adult is being played off against another.

Your expectations of discipline will of course have to be adjusted as your children grow up but the basic need for safety and civilised behaviour remain. As children become more mature it is a good idea to include them in the decision-making. They are much more likely to accept the rules if they have helped to form them and it is important for you to understand their viewpoint, too.

Keep as few rules as you possibly can. Children do not want to feel hedged about by 'do's' and 'don'ts' all the time. They need their freedom. What they have to understand is that in enjoying their freedom they cannot trample all over everyone else, thus destroying the freedon of others. Don't forget that you are the main model as far as behavioural attitudes are concerned. Shouting, arguing and inconsiderate attitudes at home give rise to the same kind of behaviour in the children. Likewise, children who are addressed politely usually respond in the same way.

You would like to help in school?

Most Headteachers welcome parental help in school. There is no better way than this of building good relationships with the staff and gaining an understanding of the complex life of the school. Children, too, love to think that Mum and Dad are part of the team and this can affect their attitudes towards school beneficially. And you will enjoy it because working with children is such fun.

Some words of advice

The Headteacher will suggest a starting-time. It is usually wise to wait until your children have really settled into school life before beginning. The Head will place you where she thinks you would be most useful, taking into account your preference and skills.

If you can manage to make your visits to school reasonably regular the teacher will be able to plan her day with your presence in mind, and you will become a valuable stand-by.

Try to develop a detached attitude towards your own children. (At least, pretend to because I know this is impossible!).

Bear in mind that teachers are always very busy, so avoid catching them for the odd chat or the exchange of incident, however tempting this is.

Ways of helping in school

There are as many different ways of helping as there are schools. Your particular school will use your help as suits it best. Here are some popular ways:

- hearing children read and giving extra help to those in difficulty. Reading to, and with children, especially where the system of individualised reading is followed (see section on reading);

- helping with demanding activities, such as sewing, woodwork, cooking, or supervising a newly-introduced game;
- helping to maintain the dressing-up stand, the wendy house, the domestic play area, or the library corner;
- on duty in the school library, keeping everything spruce and helping children find the books they need;
- using your special skills or hobbies to add interest to the daily routine. Children love to hear about the experiences of others and enjoy listening to a fresh voice;
- working with a group in the classroom, after the class-teacher has set them off on their work;
- helping with changing for physical education, games or swimming – extra help in this time-consuming chore is very much welcomed by teachers;
- helping to run after-school clubs: stamps, chess, animal care or folk-dancing;
- accompanying the class on outings and school visits, when extra adults are always needed.

These suggestions are, of course, for Dads as well as Mums. Most teachers of young children tend to be women and men in the classroom are something of a rarity and therefore highly valued. Children from one-parent families are often brought up by the mother and may not have the chance to build relationships with men, so a masculine presence is very welcome. Whether you are able to help in school or not, you should bear in mind that the teacher always has the responsibility of planning the work, explaining it to the children and starting it off. Don't be apprehensive that you might suddenly be faced with a group of children to 'teach'. Your very useful function will be to keep it all going, see that the children have what they need and help them generally along the way. In doing this you will enable the teacher to concentrate on another group without interruption.

Now for the work

Introduction

When we are thinking about children's work in school we should bear in mind several important points:

1 Young children learn through practical work. They must be doing, discussing and practising to gain understanding.
2 Children learn at different rates from each other. For this reason it is not useful to compare one with another. Progress must always be judged against a previous standard and not against other children. We must accept that children have different abilities and gifts.
3 Progress is not constant. Sometimes children seem to forge ahead by leaps and bounds; whilst at other times they seem to stand still. They have periods when they are absorbing what they have learnt and are not ready for more forward steps. Progress is affected by many other circumstances too: for example, physical health, the response to the teacher, the child's mood, the inherent difficulty of the work, happenings at home, tiredness, and so on.
4 Learning is a long, gradual process, and knowledge is amassed slowly over the years. Success is rarely achieved with startling suddenness. A long period of work usually precedes the final goal. So we must have faith in our children, and confidence in the school, in the certainty that in the end, children will learn.
5 Learning is a three-way process. It requires effort and involvement from the teacher AND the child, backed up by a strong continuous support from parents. If any of the three fail in their part, progress is held up.
6 All school activities are considered as 'work', be they art, music, basic skills, physical education, sand-play, table

games, or whatever. All are equally important to the children.

7 Feelings of anxiety, pressure and lack of confidence are quickly communicated to the children and always slow progress down; whilst praise, support and encouragement always help things on and, moreover, give the children the vital self-confidence they need to find their way through the world.

In this section of the book, I shall set out to give you some idea of how each area of the curriculum is taught, though in a book of this size this information is bound to be curtailed. The picture described will be a general one and you are certain to find different practices in many schools. Nevertheless, I hope it will give you some idea of commonly accepted approaches and you can explore from there.

Reading

What it involves

Of all the skills taught in school, reading seems to concern parents most. This is understandable since a child's ability to cope with future education and life outside school depends to a great extent on this. When mastered, reading brings great pleasure and is a key to further information, so its value is not merely utilitarian.

Reading is a difficult skill to master because it is very abstract. The children are dealing with strange shapes and symbols (called letters) often very similar to each other. When these shapes and symbols are arranged in a certain way, they represent words, which together form sentences; these, when de-coded, tell them something.

Reading depends upon:

- noticing shapes;
- noticing positions;
- memory;
- knowing plenty of words, so that the de-coding of the shapes makes sense;
- and motivation.

Children will only learn to read when they want to. The driving force in this difficult task is the desire to succeed. So those children who have learnt to love books will learn quickly. Those who have not met books at home, nor listened to stories, will not. Fortunately for teachers, most children come to school wanting, indeed expecting to learn to read, and are willing to work hard to achieve this. But some do not and here the teacher's first task is to motivate them to want to learn to read.

Reading readiness

Children are ready to learn when:

- they can talk in sentences;
- they have a wide vocabulary, and can use words well;
- when they can listen with involvement to stories;
- when they enjoy looking at books;
- when they can understand and follow simple instructions;
- when they can remember simple rhymes and little stories;
- when they can do jigsaw puzzles and shape recognition games with some success.

Many children come to school without this reading-readiness and pre-reading activities are provided to help them. Now that the importance of this work is recognised there are many exciting activities available. So don't be worried if your children are not immediately given a reading book when they start school. The teacher must check up that they are ready to learn first.

Methods of teaching reading

Visual approach or 'look and say' Many schools start with this method. It is basically a method where children learn to recognise sentences and words by picture association and where the sentences are learnt as a

Story-time. Listening is an important part of learning.

whole. The pictures act as clues at first, while the children are learning to recognise the sentence by its shape, length and general features. Then they pick out names and frequently used words and, finally, all the words in the sentence are assimilated. There will be many games to give practice in this. These activities will lead to the reading scheme, which is based on the words already learnt and illustrated by attractive pictures.

The advantage of this approach is that it makes it possible to present the children with more interesting and natural reading books, since these are not dependant on words which can be sounded out. Children quickly experience success, and can cope with the reading scheme books with confidence. A good flow of reading is established.

The phonic approach With this method children are taught the SOUND of the letters (not their names which are altogether different) and decode the word by sounding them out and merging the sounds together. For example, 'bed' will b sounded as 'b . . . e . . . d', and the childre must hear the word 'bed' from this. Many find this quite hard to do. The shape of ea letter has to be remembered and linked with its sound.

It is necessary for every child at some time to learn the letter sounds since it is obvious that they cannot learn all words b shape-recognition or association.

The teacher will introduce phonics as soon as she sees the children are ready, sometimes as a group lesson, sometimes incidentally. Again there will be plenty of attractive games to help with this work in the classroom. Phonics need to be practised constantly right through the infant/first school and on into the junior school for the rules are many and complex.

Individualised reading This is a relatively new approach to the teaching of reading and uses ordinary children's books instead of a reading scheme. The idea is that real books motivate children to read since they are more fun than reading scheme books and that they will learn in a more natural way. Tapes, silent reading, reading aloud to an adult, paired reading and group reading all play a part and much emphasis is placed on vocabulary extension. Children at the same stage of learning are gathered together for specific teaching, and visual recognition and phonics will be used as they are needed.

Involving parents in the teaching of reading Many schools now work very closely with parents in the teaching of reading. In addition to sending home reading books and suggestions of games to play, parents are invited into school to hear their children read and to work with them in other ways. This partnership of professional expertise and parental interest makes for quick success and if your school encourages this kind of involvement you are very fortunate and your children will soon become fluent readers.

Reading schemes These consist of a series of small books, which use a selected vocabulary; this is introduced gradually, as the scheme advances. Sentences start by being very simple and new words are used frequently. The books increase in difficultly as the scheme progresses.

The books must be read in strict order or the children will not be prepared for the new words they meet. Ideally, all new words should be learnt before the new book is read so that the children meet with success at once. Each reading scheme is backed up with extra materials: pictures,

games, word activities, matching games and by comprehension cards. There are many attractive schemes available and schools often use several so that the teacher can choose the scheme which suits that particular child best. Many schemes offer 'sideways' extension i.e. extra books at each stage of reading to consolidate each level. If you are reading with your children at home, either before they start school or afterwards, it is wise to avoid using the same schemes as are found in the school. This could cause problems for the teacher. Besides, your children would be bored by meeting the same books again. So inquire at the school and find out which books to avoid. You could choose easy reading books from the public library instead.

Reading all round Children see words everywhere at school – and this daily bombardment of words makes children aware of their practical uses. They come to understand that reading has a real importance in everyday life. At the same time, they absorb the words unconsciously. Reading is not confined to the period of teaching in the classroom, it is going on all the time. It is likely that, whatever system of teaching reading is used in school, most children learn from a combination of methods.

Some common worries for parents

When are they going to be given a proper reading book? Your children are probably not yet ready for a reading book. Be patient. When they do begin, having been thoroughly prepared, they will race away.

Why are they so long on the same book? This means they have been put on to the book too soon and are inadequately prepared. If this happens they will fail and become discouraged about the whole business. Perhaps you could help at home with the preparation work? Ask the teacher if you could borrow some of the equipment.

'Why is Tom only on book 3, when John is on book 5? Does it mean that he is slow?' No, it only means that he is progressing at his own speed. Never compare stages because some children learn faster, some slower, and the pace will alter from time to time – Tom possibly overtaking John later. Discourage your children from comparisons too. Reading is not a race but a gradual process of building up the skills.

'This book's too easy!' At certain stages, teachers deliberately give children books to read which are easy for them. This provides a chance for them to consolidate their gains and read fluently. If they have to struggle over every book they are not likely to develop a taste for reading.

'She's not really reading it, she knows it by heart!' Sometimes children do learn the whole book by heart and recite it proudly, swanking that they are reading. Parents get concerned about this but it is a proper and natural stage in learning to read and should not be criticised or stopped. As they progress this will come to an end. You can help them by asking them which word says 'dog' or 'house' or whatever, or how many times does 'dog' come on the page.

When will they learn the alphabet? They do not learn this at first because the letter names would confuse them. It is the sounds they need. (See chart on page 41.)

Children will learn the alphabet when they reach the stage of using a dictionary or reference books and this comes quite soon, though in a simple form. They will be familiar with the order of letters from the alphabet charts on the classroom wall. They will apply this in their own little home-made dictionaries, which they will present to the teacher when asking for a word.

Children who can read, but don't. These

reluctant readers need strong motivation and sometimes guileful persuasion.

- Try reading with them, taking turns. Also, read to them, even though they are perfectly capable of doing this for themselves. There is something about being read to, which often starts them off.
- Let them see you enjoying a good read and organise a time at the weekend when the whole family reads together. Discuss your books with each other and exchange views.
- Make sure that the children have joined the local public library and pay regular visits.
- Try setting a reading target for each week and let them fill in a chart to show their progress. Present a home-made medal if they top the chart!
- Provide books with attractive pictures, clear print and fairly short sentences; use comics to encourage them.

Guessing the words This can be a useful aid to reading, providing it is an intelligent guess. It proves that the child has understood the story and is following it with interest. Some teachers advise parents not to correct the mistake unless the word obviously does not make sense. When they have learnt the letter sounds they will use these as a guide in their guessing and you are entitled then to say, 'how can that word be "tiger", when it starts with "l"? Have another try.'

Does the teacher hear them read daily? The teacher certainly tries to do this, but there must be the odd occasion when this is impossible. This will not matter if it is only occasional, as some work involving reading is bound to take place.

Children with reading problems will be heard daily and are likely to be set extra reading activities. Once they have become fluent readers, the teacher will hear them regularly but not so frequently as before.

She will be checking up on expression and comprehension. Good readers may keep records of the books they have read, with comments on the story.

They may be required to answer questions on the plot.

Helping children with reading difficulties

These children need:

- plenty of encouragement and praise;
- daily, regular practice and extra help, with plenty of repetition;
- easy books for quick success (home-made books, comics, books with captions only are all helpful):
- help with the initial sound of the words (games like 'I Spy' can help, but remember to use the letter sound and not the name);
- to be put into the situation where they must read things for you, e.g. to find the recipe for the ginger biscuits or to read the instructions on a food packet;
- practice with writing and spelling to help reading (make your own word games – use boxes of letters and ask them to sort out muddled words, or make 3 words beginning with 'p' or with 2 syllables or ending with 'st', like 'post' – you can think up endless varieties of games which are at the same time useful);
- the confidence they gain from reading a book they read well to a younger child, or to a relative.

Hearing children read

This requires uninterrupted time and attention. Try to avoid the situation when you are listening and doing the washing-up at the same time. Children crave for, and need, your whole-hearted concentration and they really do deserve it more than the washing-up! Learning by heart is an important part of reading, so teach the traditional nursery rhymes and also their modern eqivalent, pop songs and jingles.

Should I teach my children to read before they start school?

If you have given your children plenty of pre-reading activities and if they WANT to learn to read, then do not stop them. In fact you will not be able to, they will learn regardless. Providing you do not exert pressure on them for this to happen, learning to read before school starts can only be an advantage. Some teachers object to it because they think there will be confusion over methods and approaches; but in my experience, children quickly absorb all approaches and take what they need from each. However, do be certain to tell the teacher what books your child has read. Then the teacher can start your child on a different series, or put them on to individual books straight away. It seems to me just as iniquitous to hold children back as to force them on beyond their pace.

Dyslexia

This can be described as a development disorder, which makes it difficult (though not impossible) for children to learn the basic skills of reading, writing, spelling and, sometimes, mathematics. It is a kind of hidden handicap. Dyslexic children appear to learn very unevenly, seeming very slow in some work, and exceedingly bright or quite normal in other respects. Some common characteristics are:

- poor co-ordination, for instance, difficulty in controlling a pencil, catching a ball, dealing with buttons and bows, riding a bike, etc;
- persistent difficulty in learning to read, write and spell – letters are jumbled up and often reversed, words read backwards, etc;
- persistent problems with any kind of ordering, i.e. with days of the week, or syllables of long words;
- problems with telling the time, distinguishing left and right, remembering arithmetical tables, etc;

The word 'persistent' is the keyword here because many children have problems with these aspects of learning at some time or other. Most overcome them with normal teaching and home support. Dyslexic children require special help, however. If you are worried about this, talk to the Headteacher who will link you up with your local association if considered necessary. (See address list for details.)

Do remember that not all slow-learning children are dyslexic and do not be in too much of a hurry to fasten this label on them. Talk to the Head first.

Reading for a purpose

As soon as the children have made a start on reading they are expected to use it in their school work. This provides an added stimulus since they cannot really manage without it. They must read their work-cards, instructions in their maths books and, later on, their text books; they must learn to use reference books and dictionaries; they must understand all they have read in order to carry out the task in hand. One of the basic things children must learn in the infant/first school, is how to be able to follow through a piece of work without recourse to the teacher and using their reading skills plays an important part in this.

Reading records

Teachers keep a record of books read by each child, with useful comments on any problems encountered. A checklist of phonic sounds and irregular words may be kept, with notes on comprehension and fluency. These records are passed on when the child moves to another class so that the next teacher can benefit from them and add to them. Most schools test reading regularly, using diagnostic tests which identify particular difficulties.

Learning to use a reference book

Around about six years of age children learn the alphabet by heart and begin to use a real dictionary and reference books, for looking up information on their own. This does not come naturally to children and has to be taught gradually, starting with very simple, clearly organised books which do not overwhelm them with too much information. If you could help your children over this hurdle at home, you will be doing them a great service. Show them:

- how to find the right letter section, using their knowledge of the alphabet; how to decide whether the word is likely to be at the beginning, in the middle or at the end of the book. Little children often start the laborious process of turning the pages over one by one, hoping to arrive soon at the letter they need;
- how to pick out the precise bit of information they need. Children tend to copy out the whole entry at first and it is crucial that they come to understand that this is not always necessary. They must select the facts they need.

Practice:

- looking up names in an address book;
- looking up telephone numbers;
- using an index;
- finding page numbers;
- finding cooking recipes;
- looking up a flower name in the book;
- using an encyclopedia.

Language work

Spoken language

Language is the means whereby we make relationships with others, share our ideas and influence the actions of those around us. The spoken language is especially important when children begin to write their ideas down – as news, a story or an account. How can we expect them to do this if they cannot talk clearly in sentences and only have a very limited vocabulary?

Here are some ways a strong emphasis is placed on expressing ideas in speech in infant/first schools:

- through working in groups (with the teacher joining in, using the extending vocabulary the work may include, to encourage a sensible exchange);
- at newstime and storytelling time;
- all class sessions, when a prime part of the teacher's task is to introduce the new vocabulary the work demands;
- through drama, rhymes, poetry and listening to stories;
- through free play – e.g. in the wendy house, with bricks, in dressing up etc. – to develop language in a natural way;
- visitors, functions and formal greetings. Children like greeting visitors and showing them round their school.

Handwriting

This is a laborious process for young children, involving the control of many muscles, especially the fine muscles of first finger and thumb. It is not a natural activity for children and needs strong motivation, with constant practice and regular teaching.

Do not expect too much at first; the writing will be wobbly and erratic and certainly won't 'sit on the line'. A great deal of concentration, and control of the eye, arm and finger muscles is involved. This

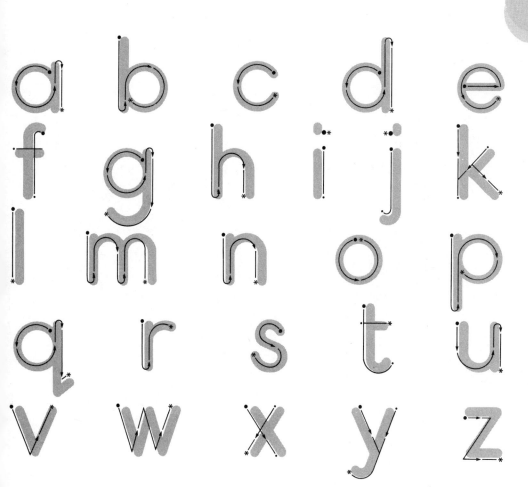

takes time to master and needs teaching, to show how each letter is formed.

It is no good leaving children to gouge out the letters as they think fit. The correct starting point and direction of each letter is one of the most vital aspects of the work and requires work with the teacher to become automatic.

There are of course variations in approach to handwriting in schools. Some teach the plain print letters first, for example:

a h

Others introduce the letters with a 'flick' in preparation for joined writing later on, for example:

a h

It is wise for you to find out the practice in your particular school, so that you can help reinforce it at home.

Infant schools do not usually teach joined writing (cursive writing), preferring to wait until the printing is clear and the letters well-formed. Children often reach this stage by the end of the infant school. In first schools, cursive writing is sometimes taught in the final year. Although capital letters are used in names, days, months and places, from the start, they are not taught as such until later on, when some punctuation is expected.

Teachers often take handwriting as a class lesson, forming the letters on the blackboard at the same time as the children. Individual practice is also carried out in which writing practice workbooks, writing cards, tracing, writing patterns and over-writing are all used.

Writing can be an enjoyable experience, once the initial difficulties are overcome.

Left and right-handedness There is no attempt to pursuade a left-handed child to use the right hand these days. The teacher needs to know if your children have this characteristic so that she can think about seating, about left-handed scissors, and so on. Sometimes it is quite tricky to decide whether children are left-handed or not, as they seem to use both hands equally. Do not push them either way; it will soon become clear which is the predominant hand. (Left-handed tools can be bought now; see 'Anything Left-handed' in the address list.)

Spelling

This is closely linked with reading and writing and is an essential tool for all written work. Spelling has to be taught in the same way as handwriting; it doesn't just happen, except for the fortunate few.

I am sure you would not expect the teachers to nag your children about spelling when they first start writing. This is a formidable task in itself, without being bothered all the time about spelling. What is important at this stage is the pleasure experienced and the confidence gained in the achievement of a difficult piece of work. The teacher will make sure that the children know where to look for help; at word-lists, charts, labels, etc. So you will not find that spelling looms large during the first term or two at school.

The English language is one of the most difficult for spelling because it is so irregular. Take a look at 'bow' and 'bough', or 'half', 'scarf' and 'laugh' for example. Spelling presents problems for children but it is dealt with gradually, more emphasis being placed on it as the children progress through the school. They have to learn to use the phonic sounds, the double sounds, ('ee', 'sh', 'ay', for example) and the vast collection of irregular words that are in common use. All children need teaching, practice and revision in this work. Most schools make an overall plan to ensure that the spelling rules are covered. There will be plenty of material in the classroom to help the children: word-games, workcards, matching sets, Word-Makers (see page 41), and so on. The children may bring home a few words from time to time, especially as they reach the top end of the school. (See the section 'Helping at home' at the end of this chapter.)

Correcting the spelling at school Many parents get worried about this, because the approach has changed since they were at school when their books were given back to them covered with the teacher's red pencil! At this stage, you will not find this. A more positive approach is likely to be taken. First, the misspelt word will be pointed out, but not every word will be corrected; only those words that it is reasonable to expect the children to know. It is far better for them to use an exciting or unusual word, misspelt, than to avoid using it because they cannot spell it. Secondly, the children will be asked to put the words right themselves, using the word-lists and a rubber. This will not blemish their work and, moreover, will encourage them to look first next time. Don't be surprised if, when they reach the stage of writing proper stories, the spelling goes 'haywire'. Children become so engrossed in the plot of their story that the spelling tends to become careless, even if they have had no problems previously. The handwriting may also suffer. There comes a time, of course, when this is tackled. The teacher will choose her time wisely, so that she does not spoil the children's delight in their newly-acquired skill.

Persistent difficulties If, after a reasonable time at school, your children seem to have real problems with spelling, ask the class-teacher how best you can help at home. She will probably lend you some of the school materials to work through with your children and suggest other ways of helping, too. It is important that this gets sorted out, before junior school, when more emphasis is likely to be placed on account-writing. Check your children's hearing and vision, since any defect in these can affect spelling.

Written work

This is different from handwriting, which is only a tool for written work. Handwriting concentrates on how you write; written work on what you write and the clarity with which you express it. It is as well to notice this difference right away, so that you know where to place the emphasis when your children bring home a piece of work for you to admire. In stories, it is the ideas, the sentence construction and the use of words which you look for; the handwriting and spelling come second.

There are two kinds of written work in school:

creative writing which stems from the imagination and encourages a colourful use of words to create a mood; into this category come stories, descriptions and poems.

factual writing where information and relevant facts must be selected and expressed clearly in sentences. This occurs in news-writing and simple account-writing about events or the project. As the children move through the educational system this kind of writing becomes increasingly important, since it occurs in almost every subject.

Two significant points to bear in mind about all written work are:

1 The ideas must stem from the children from the very beginning. Help for ideas, suggestions for words, different ways of starting will all be discussed beforehand, but the actual ideas should be the children's. With this emphasis, the awful moan of 'I don't know what to say!' is less likely to arise. Copying the teacher's story from the blackboard too, is useless if the aim is to initiate children into writing down their own ideas.

2 All children work to their own level. The ability to write develops slowly in most cases, and at different speeds in different children. It is affected by motivation, reading skills, and the physical control of the pencil, as well as by previous experience with books, and much else.

How it is introduced at school Children are led into written work gradually. One of the most popular ways of doing this is through the children's own personal news, where the motivation is already strong. The stages in this are:

- telling their news;
- drawing a picture and the teacher writes a sentence with it – at the child's dictation;
- the same process but with the child over-writing – and later copying the written sentence;
- finally, the children find their own words and write independently. Concurrently, other activities will take place, such as mapping pictures to words; a joint class effort, when a common experience is recorded by a contribution from each child or focused writing, where all the children write about one subject, e.g. their pets. There are many ways of motivating the children in this demanding skill.

Writing is not a natural process for young children; they would far rather tell us about an event than write it down. We adults know that the ability to write well is essential for all future education and because of this we introduce the work early, to cover the basic groundwork and accustom children to it. But we cannot expect children to appreciate this point. Many of them are reluctant writers. They will tackle it purposefully if they see a reason for it, like keeping a bird record, or writing a letter to Oxfam, or a story for the class collection. The completed work should be seen and admired by others, not hidden away in an exercise book. This is why you

"Me and my friends on the climbing frame"
by James

will see so much written work displayed in infant/first schools.

Once they are over the first difficulties, children come to enjoy this means of communicating their ideas. You will gain much pleasure from your children's written efforts and probably some surprises too. For children see the the world in a different way from adults; everything is exciting and fresh to them and this often comes through in their written work. When you are presented with this, remember that it is the content of the work you should comment on first, not the handwriting or spelling. It is a bonus if these are also satisfactory.

Finding the words One of the main problems in written work is finding the words. The more independent children become in this, the more they gain confidence in their ability. Round the classroom you will see some of these aids:

- names of all the class-members, teachers and helpers;
- lists of family names – auntie, brother, etc;

- word-lists relating to a particular subject – the project or maths;
- all equipment, storage areas, exhibitions, models, etc. labelled;
- timetables, menus, calendars, weather-chart, days and months;
- some suggestions for exciting words to use, to add atmosphere to writing;
- story beginnings, to inspire a different start;
- a list of favourite story characters – witch, princess, astronaut, and so on.
- reading books, home-made dictionaries and Sentence-Maker.

The 'Sentence-Maker' is a very useful piece of equipment. It provides support when children are struggling with learning to read. The scheme is called 'Breakthrough to Literacy' (produced by Longman Group) and has several parts to it – the Sentence-Maker, two Word-Makers and the Project Folder. Also available is a well-thought out Word Book. The Sentence-Maker is a three-leaved folder, designed to hold a specially-chosen vocabulary; these are words frequently used by children, when they start reading or writing. Each word is slotted into a pocket in the folder, on which is printed the same word, for easy replacement. With this folder comes a plastic stand. Children select the words they need, place them upright in the stand and read their own sentence. A full-stop is provided, which the children quickly learn to use. There are other cunning refinements – for example, no plurals are given, the 's' or 'es' must be added by the children; the word endings 'ing',' ed' and' n't' can be added to change words too – for example, jump + ing give jumping, and play + ed makes played, while did + n't gives didn't.

They are learning quite complex grammatical rules without even realising it, from the very start. Children love using the Sentence-Maker because the sentences and stories they make are their own and they are physically handling the words. No tiresome writing need be involved at first. Also, they meet with immediate success.

The Word-Maker works on the same principle, using letters and double sounds instead of words. It is a very useful aid to spelling.

The confused writer Once children become confident in their ability to write, ideas stream out in profusion. Sometimes, in their enthusiasm, ideas become muddled, sentences and phrases run into each other, words are left out, the spelling is disastrous, and so on. What should you do about this? One effective way is to ask the child to read it back to you; usually this proves impossible, even for the author! This is when you can make your point about all the 'horrid little details'. Care must be taken, however, not to cause the marvellous flow of ideas to seize up altogether, because it is this flow which brings success later.

Children with persistent difficulties Most children find writing a bit of a problem at some time, but there are some who have real difficulty with it, and come to dread it at school; every activity seems to be spoilt

by having to 'write about it'. In this case, get the advice of the teacher on how best you can help at home.

She can tell you exactly where the problem lies. On a one-to-one basis, at home, you are likely to be able to give the extra help required and, more importantly, can give support and encouragement.

Helping at home

Reading Remember, whenever you are helping your children with reading or spelling, it is the letter sound, not the name, which is important.

a as in 'apple', not 'ay'
b as in 'bird', not 'bee'
c as in 'curve', not 'see'
d as in 'dirt', not 'dee'
e as in 'egg', not 'ee'
f as in 'firm', not 'eff'
g as in 'girl', not 'jee'
h as in 'hurt', not 'aitch'
i as in 'ink', not 'eye'
j as in 'jerk', not 'jay'
k as in 'kerb', not 'kay'
l as in 'learn', not 'ell'
m as in 'mark', not 'emm'
n as in 'nurse', not 'enn'
o as in 'ox', not 'oh'
p as in 'purse', not 'pea'
qu as in 'quick', not 'queue'
r as in 'run', nor 'are'
s as in 'serve', not 'ess'
t as in 'turn', not 'tee'
u as in 'under', not 'you'
v as in 'verse', not 'vee'
w as in 'work', not 'double-you'
x as in 'fox', not 'ex'
y as in 'year', not 'why'
z as in 'zebra', not 'zed'

Spoken language The best way to help your children to grow into confident, articulate children, with a wide vocabulary and a skill in forming sentences is through talking. There is so much you can do to help at home, in the car, on those boring shopping expeditions. Here are some suggestions:

1 Make a point of including your children in meal-time conversations, especially when you have visitors. They need to be made to feel part of the conversation, their opinions sought and their answers listened to.
2 Practise the 'formal' codes of behaviour – expect them to say 'please' and 'thank you' and to greet your visitors properly.
3 Encourage playing at telephone conversations, role-playing in dressing up and all 'pretending' games. These are valuable for stimulating the imagination and motivating speech.
4 Play games with words, such as:
   • describing an object without naming it. The children have to guess the object.
   • finishing a phrase – you start the phrase, and they must finish it, e.g. 'a creepy ...' 'house/story/wood';
   • telling a story, describing everything as 'nice' or using any over-worked word. For example, 'There was once a nice boy, who lived in a nice house, in a nice town.' The children must find some more exciting words to fit in.

Handwriting Before children start at school they need lots of practice for their arm, hand and finger muscles. Painting, modelling and scribbling are good for this. Don't worry about paper because children will happily use newspaper or the backs or old Christmas cards. Give them thick pencils and chunky wax crayons, large paintbrushes and thick paint. At this stage they are learning the nature of the tools and how to control them. Using constructional toys, like plastic Meccano or Lego, also helps to develop the vital finger-control. Some more specific ways of helping are:

   • colouring-in – introduces control as the outline needs to be observed;
   • holding the pencil – probably at first, the children will hold the pencil clutched firmly in the fist and scribble using the whole arm. Try, at the proper moment, to show them how to hold the pencil correctly, between the first finger and thumb.
   • directional activities, or 'taking the line for a walk': letters are formed from top to bottom, whilst the words flow from left to right, so both directional terms need to be known; (the terms 'left' and 'right' are very useful to know – try teaching them by shaking hands every morning, saying at the same time, 'the right hand, of course!')
   • tracing, using large clear pictures with not too many lines. Clip the tracing paper to the picture, or words, as it tends to slip around in a frustrating way;
   • writing patterns to help in pencil control and directional flow – they are lovely done in paint, too (start at the dot and follow the arrow);

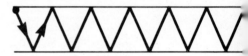

the 'up-down' pattern

the 'bounce' pattern

   • making a name-card for the children, using a piece of cardboard and large print. They will enjoy tracing it and copying it;
   • showing them how to form the letters, so that they do not have to re-learn them later. The chart on page **35** will show you where to start and which direction to follow;

- encouraging them to use their new skill. Let them write the shopping list, a 'no milk today' note, jam labels, reminder note to Dad, and so on. This will give a real meaning to all their efforts.

Spelling No special work needs to be done before the children start school, since they are not ready for such detail yet. It is a help, both with reading and spelling, if children can hear the initial sounds of words; that 'dog' begins with 'd' (not 'dee'!), or 'table' with 't' (not 'tee!'). Place three toys – a ball, a car, and a teddy – on the table. Ask the children to give you the toy beginning with 'b' and so on. Or ask them to touch something in the room beginning with 'd'. You'll think of many variations to help them hear the sounds. Everything must be fun, all the time; as soon as it becomes tiresome, stop doing it.

Once spelling has started at school, you can help a great deal at home.

1 Work with them, to learn any words sent home. Struggling with spellings by yourself is not much fun. A box of letters will help.
2 Play some of the popular word-games with them, such as Scrabble, Can-U-Go or Lexicon. You may have to simplify the rules at first.
3 Make sure that they have a simple dictionary and understand how to use it.
4 Give them a book of simple crossword puzzles, and help them to do these.

Written work Infant and first school children often do not want to write at home – they do plenty of writing during their daily lessons! The best way to help during term-time is through conversation or reading to them. Have you tried reading poetry to them? Young children respond to the rhythm of this and they begin to appreciate how words can 'colour' a piece of writing.

Holiday ideas It is a good idea to keep in practice during the long school holidays.

Try launching a holiday diary, with a lovely large book and a new box of crayons. Children enjoy writing about themselves and what they have done. It need only be a sentence or two. Include everything that might be relevant in the book – postcards, tickets, sweet-wrappers, programmes and each entry can be explained with a short phrase or sentence, e.g. 'This is the train ticket', or 'On the way I had a Mars Bar'.

Children who have a flair for writing sometimes enjoy writing a 'real' story-book, setting it out in chapters and illustrating it. At school they do not always get sufficient time for this, so the holidays provide a golden opportunity.

Make a collection of something interesting to the children – shells, pictures of pop-stars or cars, or wild flowers. You will need a little corner for display, or a book to mount the exhibits in – some writing is sure to be involved.

Writing letters is a way of keeping in practice. Children love receiving letters, and will quickly come to see that if you write a letter, you often get an answer.

In all this work you will need a good supply of words, so show the children where they can find them. A good idea is to print them clearly in the back of the book they are using, in alphabetical order.

Mathematics

Introduction

Over the past few years many changes have been made in primary school mathematics and the speed with which this has happened sometimes worries parents, who feel that they do not know what is going on. The curriculum has widened out to include many topics which formerly were not taught until grammar school and some which were not included at all. 'Maths' is about real things, in the real world. It is of great significance that our children understand this; they must learn what maths is for and how they can use it themselves. So they must have first-hand practical experiences in real situations. They must discuss this work with each other and with the teacher, in order to learn the special language of mathematics. Formerly, so many children disliked maths, and even though they could 'do sums' in a parrot fashion, having learnt the trick of it, when they were presented with a problem to solve they would despair. We want to teach our children to understand and enjoy maths and to feel confident that they can use it, whilst at the same time keeping a firm hold on all the basic number facts, the essential tools of mathematics.

The use of calculators and computers in the real world has led to these machines being introduced into schools. It is rare in the outside world for complicated 'sums' to be worked out on paper, but it is still very important for children to understand and be able to work out the four rules in arithmetic. Although the machine will do the sum for you, it cannot decide which rule to use so the understanding is vitally important. I do

Weighing the guinea-pig. Practical maths in a real situation brings involvement and understanding.

These boys are practicing work on money. The box of coins is there, if they need it.

not want to confuse you with too much detail about mathematics. You will, no doubt, be invited to attend meetings at school, where the Head will talk about his or her particular methods and curriculum. It is important to you to understand the basic approach to be found in most schools and to see how, from all this work, a bank of mathematical experiences and facts are gradually built up to form the foundation of future work.

The classroom scene

Practical work –e.g. weighing, measuring, filling and emptying containers, counting bricks, matching number symbols to groups of objects.

Discussion – between the children themselves and between the teacher and the children, either as a class, in a group or as an individual. Discussion helps to clarify the work for the children and the teacher discovers if the pupils have really understood the maths.

Recording – shows the children that a practical situation can be translated into the language and symbols of maths, helps to fix the facts in their minds and teaches them the importance of keeping a record.

Further practice –work which requires the application of what the children have learnt.

An example of practical work There is only space here to give one example of what is meant by 'practical work'. This shows you how the actual maths is derived from what, at first sight, appears to be playing.

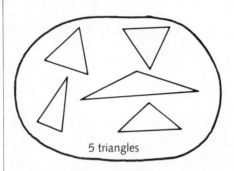

5 triangles

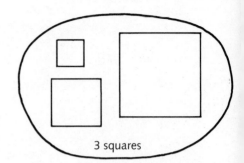

3 squares

Materials used: a pile of triangular and square shapes, previously sorted by the teacher.

First task: to sort the shapes into two sets, according to the property of shape. The children sort them out and draw round them on a large piece of paper, labelling each set.

Some questions the teacher may ask:

- How many shapes altogether?
- What are the shapes called?
- How many triangles? How many squares?
- Which set has the most members, squares or triangles? How can you find out? Pair them up in two's and that will tell you.
- How many more triangles than squares?
- How many fewer squares than triangles?
- Can you tell me, from looking at the work, what 5 and 3 make? So what is three more than 5? What about 5 plus 3? What about 3 plus 5?
- How many sides has a triangle? How many corners?
- How many sides has a square? How many corners?

- Do you notice anything about the sides of the square – that they are all the same length?

From this work, the children will have experienced the following maths:

- sorting, counting, placing in pairs;
- recognition and names of the two shapes plus some of their properties;
- the terms 'more than', 'less than', 'altogether';
- practice in using the number symbols 5, 3, 8 and the signs +, −, = may be introduced;
- some number facts: $5 + 3 = 8$
$$3 + 5 = 8$$
$$8 - 5 = 3$$
$$8 - 3 = 5$$

(The relationships in these numbers will be noticed by some children.)

- the idea that real objects, i.e. the shapes, can be represented on paper by a drawing and number symbols. The real situation has been translated into an abstract recording, using the language of mathematics.

Further experience will be given along the same lines, possibly asking the children to sort the shapes according to their colour.

The type of activity will be the same but the results different. After this the children will practice these number bonds orally and in their workbooks; the teach will find ways of reinforcing and revisin the work.

What will they cover in maths? This of course varies slightly from school to schoc

Work on sets. Discussion with the teacher is an essential part of all mathematics.

but here is a likely list.

- counting, and the number line, up to and beyond 100;
- a knowledge of the number bonds, especially those of 10;
- counting in 2s, 3s, 4s, 5s, 10s etc, as a preparation for learning the tables by rote;

  an understanding of our system of notation – the use of 10s;
- facts about numbers – odds and evens, prime numbers, square numbers etc;

  work in the four rules, up to hundreds, tens and units;
- work in sets, sorting, belonging to a set, subsets, etc;
- work in measurement of length, weight, capacity, volume, and area;

- work in plane and solid shapes, some geometry in connection with these;
- work with money, coin recognition, bills, change;
- telling the time; minutes, hours, days, weeks, months;
- the use of all the equipment involved in the above work – balances, metresticks, selecting suitable weights, etc;
- work with statistics, charts, graphs, maps, etc.

All this work will involve traditional sums and a knowledge of tables.

The early stage Here are some examples of the kind of maths you may see in your children's books when they first start school.

47

Verbal labelling

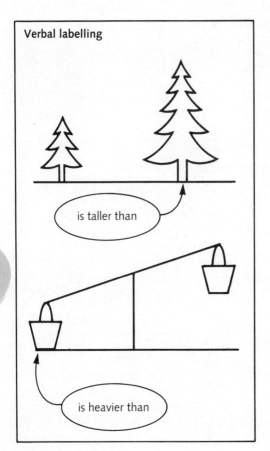

is taller than

is heavier than

Graphs and charts

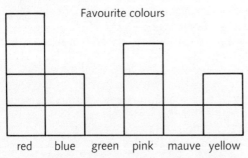

Favourite colours

red   blue   green   pink   mauve   yellow

This lends itself to many useful mathematical questions:

- How many children like red best? How many children were asked altogether?
- How many more children prefer pink to yellow?

Some more advance mathematics
Continue this pattern.

$17 + 6 =$ ☐

$27 + 6 =$ ☐

$37 + 6 =$ ☐

☐

☐

Fill in the chart, to show how you would build up the sums of money.

	50p	20p	10p	5p	2p	1p
88p	I	I	I	I	I	I
65p	I		I	I		
74p						
93p						
99p						

Colour in three-quarters – ¾ – of these shapes.

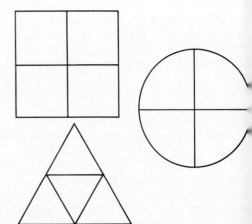

48

Recording the work When you look at your children's maths workbooks, you will notice that they are recording their work in very different ways. This may be confusing to you. Formerly, we used to write sums down in one or two ways only. Nowadays, children are taught to express their maths findings in a variety of ways – all of them mathematically sound.

The mathematical symbols A greater variety of symbols are used, in addition to the familar ones.

$$+ \quad - \quad \div \quad \times \quad =$$

Here are some symbols which may be new to you

$\neq$ means 'is not equal to' e.g. $2 (4) \neq 9$

$>$ means 'is greater than' e.g. $13 > 12 \div 4$

$<$ means 'is less than' e.g. $2 < 7$

$\emptyset$ is referred to as zero, nought, nothing, or an empty set.

$\equiv$ is described as 'is exactly the same as'

$\subset$ stands for 'is a sub-set of'

$\not\subset$ stands for 'is not a sub-set of'

The four 'rules' of addition, subtraction, multiplication and division are not always recorded in the traditional way, though this is practised too. Here are some examples:

$(2, 6) = 8$ means 2 add $6 = 8$

Take away 2

$7 \quad 8$ means $7 - 2 = 5$
$6 \quad 5$ means $6 - 2 = 4$
$0 \quad 4$ means $10 - 2 = 8$

$2 (4) = 8$ means $2 \times 4 = 8$

$$\frac{10}{2} = 5 \quad \text{means } 10 \div 2 = 5$$

Mathematical problems are met in practical daily life, and the teacher will use these happenings to show the children how to 'translate' the real situation into mathematical symbols.

Sometimes the children may be asked which symbol to use, in certain situations. For example: 'I have 4 roses and 6 daisies; altogether I have 10 flowers'. What kind of sum is that? Which symbol do I use? Can you write the sentence down?

This is very valuable practice and one you could give your children at home. Use small numbers and always provide the answer, because the object is to 'translate' the sentence into mathematics, not to work out the answer.

Do not let these new approaches to maths worry you. If your children haven't already explained things to you, ask the teacher, who will be delighted to find you interested. You can feel envious of your children, who are being taught in such an exciting and realistic way, especially if you were always bothered by maths when you were at school.

Some common queries from parents

Do they do maths every day? The answer will probably be 'yes' and often in more ways than one. The children may find themselves doing 'formal' maths in the morning and enjoying a practical experience in the afternoon. They may not realise that they are working at maths; to them, it is just an enjoyable activity.

Do they do 'sums' as we used to? They are introduced to these either as they meet them in the maths scheme or as they need them in practical work or when the teacher sees that they are ready, having already worked on the number bonds needed. Because they have been thoroughly prepared by practical work and oral practice, they will not need to do pages and pages of these sums, all of the same kind.

How do they set out addition with 'carrying', and subtraction with 'borrowing'?

$$\begin{array}{r} 26 \\ +\ 15 \\ \hline 41 \\ \scriptstyle 1 \end{array}$$

Start adding with the units. 6 + 5 makes 11. 11 is 1 ten and 1 unit. The unit goes in proper column, and the ten is placed in its column.

$$\begin{array}{r} 50 \\ -\ 19 \\ \hline \end{array}$$

In this sum, it is convenient to think of the 50 as 40/10, or forty-ten. It is exactly the same number.

Then the sum becomes:

$$\begin{array}{r} {}^{4}\cancel{5}{}^{1}0 \\ -\ 19 \\ \hline 31 \end{array}$$

and work can proceed as usual. No 'borrowing' and 'paying back', please! it doesn't make sense, whereas splitting the number up does.

Do they still learn their tables? Yes they do, but they do not learn to chant them at such an early age as formerly. They will learn the number facts first, and then practice counting in 2s, 5s, and 10s, and other groups. They will be able to tell you that 2 sets of 6 make 12, long before they can recite the 6 times table. The systemising, or learning by rote, of the tables will be emphasised at the top end of the school, and will be revised in the junior school. You do not need to worry if your childen do not know all their tables before they reach the junior school.

What about the very bright, or backward child? Since the children work in groups, a their own level, there is no problem here. The very high flyer can work individually, following a specially planned course. The only danger for these children is boredom, which will set in if they are not sufficiently extended. There are usually plenty of extension activities in the classroom.

Those children who are slow in starting can receive the extra help they need. Equipment and materials in the classroom are there for children to use as they require them. Workcards supplement the maths scheme and provide more practice where i is needed. Children progress at different rates, according to their ability, powers of concentration, their willingness to listen an become involved, as well as their emotion maturity. If your children seem to be havin persistent problems, first check up with th class-teacher on their classroom behaviou and work attitudes. If all is not as it shoulc be, deal with this – no child can learn whi playing about. You could do a great job a home, fixing the number bonds and table and may be able to borrow games from school for this purpose.

Preparing the way at home

It seems to me important that you do thin about this, before your children start school. Just consider the enormous stress we place on pre-school activities with words, speech and stories, in the development of language, and compare this with the preparation we give to mathematics. We seem to think of this as mystical subject, only to be tackled by teachers in school. But if you stop to think moment, you'll see that maths is all arour

you in your daily life, if you can recognise it. So try to develop the skill, used so well by teachers, of seeing maths in everything. For instance:

- count everything
  . . . the stairs as you go up,
  . . . the trees in the park,
  . . . the bricks in the tower;
  when you are setting the table, ask relevant questions:
  How many people will be sitting down?
  Have we got enough chairs?
  Here are some forks, are there enough?
- turn out your purse occasionally and let the children sort the money;
- put a price on something and let them select the right coin (this must always be an exact coin at this stage);
- when carrying the shopping, ask which basket is heaviest. Is yours too heavy for you? Take something out and put it in

the other one. Is that lighter?
- let them pour out the milk or squash, suggesting the glass should be half-full or nearly full;
- share out the sweets, so that you each have the same, or so that the children have two more than you or one less, etc;
- get them to time the egg boiling, recognise the time for a television programme, for bedtime, when a parent comes home etc;
- rhymes and jingles are much loved by children. There are some good ones for teaching numbers:
  Two little dicky-birds sat upon a wall. . .
  One red engine, puffing down the track. . .
  One, two, buckle my shoe. . .
  Ten little squirrels sat on a tree . . .

Repeat them frequently, so that the children can join in and act them out, for fun.

Cooking presents marvellous chances:

- doling out the ingredients in cup or spoon measures brings in counting, filling and capacity;
- the size of various bowls;
- the number of cakes made;
- the size and weight of a large cake;
- the number of eggs.

Do not try to use kitchen scales with young children – use spoonfuls or egg-cups as a measure.

Making patterns has a lot to do with maths and you can use bricks, stones, sticks, etc. for this. Patterns can be made according to shapes, size or colour, the important point being that the unit of pattern is repeated. Make patterns with crayons and paint as well.

Play counting games, such as Ludo and Snakes and Ladders. Count collections of stones, shells, buttons etc. The children should TOUCH each item as they count, to make sure they don't race ahead with their counting. (This is very important. Parents often teach children to count by reciting the number names only, which does not give them any idea of the quality of each number.)

Once you get the idea, you will find endless opportunities at home. You will be working in ideal circumstances, with plenty of time and on a one-to-one basis. Of course, you will have to start the activities off and make a point of using all the mathematical words that are bound to come in. Here are some you are sure to use

up, down, inside, outside, in front of, behind, opposite, left, right, over, under the one after, corner, edge, line, curve, straight, large, small, tall, heavy, rough,

draw a set of your friends.

Clare   Geraldine   Carinne

I have 3 friends.

52

smooth, and all the comparatives of these – taller than, fewer than, as many as, etc. – how much, cost, coin, order, match, space, fit, fold, whole, full, empty, measure, yesterday, tomorrow, today, morning, afternoon, evening, hour, half-hour.

If your children arrive at school knowing and using at least some of these words correctly, they will have made a great start.

If you do try your hand at the pre-maths work, choose your moment carefully. A dreary day when the walk in the park has to be cancelled is a much better time than when your children are already engrossed in their own play. Stop the activity the moment concentration flags – and well before boredom sets in. It must always be fun and never a chore. Don't worry if your children seem not to respond to these mathematical ploys; just continue to talk numbers with them whenever the opportunity arises. They will meet these kind of experiences when they first start at school and they may then feel more prepared to go along with it. Children do not mature at the same rate and some will be eager for these kinds of experiences long before others show any interest.

Back-up after school has started

Once your children have started school there is much you can do to support them.

1 Continue with the 'maths with everything' approach, especially during the school holidays.
2 Help them with any work they are given to do at home; it is always difficult for young children to learn things by themselves.
3 Share your children's enthusiasm in the work. Children are likely to come home full of some exciting maths they have done and it is an anti-climax if you don't respond.
4 Practice counting in 2s, 3s, 5s and 10s. Use real objects whenever you can, pushing aside the relevant groups as you count.

5 Organise some holiday activities, for fun. For example: count the number of cars which pass your house between certain times, say, from 10.00 to 10.30. Prepare (or, better still, let them prepare) a chart for each day and let them tick off the cars as they pass. Make a block graph at the end of the week to show the results. Let the children invent questions to ask about the results:
   ● Which day saw the most cars?
   ● Which was the busiest day? Why do you think this is?
   ● How many more cars on Monday than Friday?

Children love this kind of record-keeping and you can vary it, according to where you live.
6 Maths from the children themselves is very popular. Compare body measurement, using string; compare hand-spans and strides. How many strides do they take from the front door to the back? How many does big brother take?
7 Have fun with dice – try making a record of the times each number turns up. Which turns up the most times? Which the least? Which not at all?

Computers and other technical aids in the primary school

The use of computers and other forms of technology is bound to increase in schools with the current emphasis on the need for these skills. Most primary schools have at least one computer. All primary school children of a suitable age and stage are likely to have access to them. They can become very skilled in handling them and in gaining some idea of what they can do. At school they are sensibly used on the whole, not only to teach the children how to handle the machines but, more importantly, to supplement the basic teaching. There are programmes available for all ages and

Working with the computer. The pleasure derived from this is clearly evident.

classroom; real experiences, discussion, an inter-action with other children and the teachers must always come first. However is an essential skill to learn and can provide help and stimulation in the classroom. The computer is often used with the printer, fo recording children's stories and other written work. They type their stories on th screen, amend any spelling mistakes, then see the finished work emerge on the printer. This is an exciting development an can greatly encourage children with writin or spelling problems. Children certainly enjoy working with them and some will learn from the computer, when all else seems to fail.

Other technical equipment used very successfully in the primary school are sets c headphones, in conjunction with a taped story or particular piece of information. A group of children can work together in thi way, listening to a story, whilst following i in their books. Table and number facts car be strengthened and tested, using a speci tape made by the teacher, linked to a box of maths equipment. In large classes, of mixed ability, these aids to learning can be very helpful.

B.B.C. and I.T.V. television programme are much used in schools, either as programmes in their own right or as a starter or back-up to a project, or to reinforce the basic skills.

abilities, from games with robots to those which help children to learn table facts, spelling, history and geography facts and right through to more advanced ideas in science, mathematics and reasoning. All computer work encourages logic, because instructions must be given in strict sequence.

Their successful use in schools depends upon:

- a good computer expert on the staff;
- a wise choice of programmes, since not all are educationally viable;
- a sensible allocation of computer time.

In my opinion, computers should not become a dominant feature in the primary

Creative work

What it comprises and its importance

Under this heading comes:

- all art and craft – painting, modelling, collage, drawing, printing, pattern and frieze making, junk modelling, etc;
- all musical activities – singing, moving music, percussion, listening to music, playing recorders, etc;
- all forms of drama – acting, miming, verse-speaking, dressing-up, listening

The drama session encourages all children to join in, and can help the shy or tense child to gain self-confidence.

poetry, finger plays, reciting rhymes and jingles;
- woodwork, cooking and all forms of needlework.

These creative activities are the ones your children enjoy most at school. The question, "What did you do at school today?" usually brings the answer, 'painting' or 'I made a model of a dinosaur' or 'I played the drum'. You could be forgiven for thinking that nothing else ever seems to happen! Children remember best what they enjoy most, and these creative activities are so satisfying to them that they carry the thought of them home – as well as the results: the painting, the space creature, the rock-cakes or the table-mat. I know that you will duly admire these offerings, appreciating the fact that your children need you to share in their pride of creation.

Children need teaching in the skills of creative activity, just as much as in any other subject. Creative work is among the most essential of all aspects introduced at school, for these reasons:

- it provides an outlet for tensions and stress;
- it enables them to express what they feel about their experiences, through their senses;
- it can open up new sources of interest to the children and can often reveal a talent which would otherwise not be discovered;
- it gives an opportunity to learn to use essential tools, such as handling scissors, using glue, paintbrushes, hammers, scrapers, needle and thread, pincers and staplers – all essential in everyday life, as well as making it easier for children to

cope with science and technical subjects later on in school;

- most importantly, it gives enormous pleasure to the creator.

When do they do creative work?

The frequence of the occurrence of woodwork, sewing and cookery will probably depend on the extra help that is available for the supervision required. Music and drama occur regularly. Art and craft are available to the children as part of their work (illustrating stories, news and sentences), during periods of free choice, as an option when work is finished, as part of a class-project, and so on. Visual illustration in any form is considered a valid way of recording an experience or a fact. The teacher will try to see that all children have

The frog is jumping – Jeremy aged 5.

The recorder session. These 6 year-olds are learning musical notation, as well as the recorder.

plenty of creative experiences over a period of time.

Music making

Group singing and movement to music are much enjoyed and are valuable as a means of self-expression and for promoting self-confidence. Infant/first school children will have the experience of playing the percussion instruments – drums, bells, xylophones, tambourines, clappers and rhythm-sticks – and this is one of the most popular forms of music-making. Children love rhythm and respond naturally to it. They find great pleasure in making patterns of sound with the other children.

An excellent way of introducing the children to playing an intrument is for them to take up the recorder. They will need to practise it at home. At first, the sound of this is excruciating, but I beg you to put up with it, in anticipation of the lovely sounds that will eventually emerge! Learning any instrument requires determination and patience, so try to find something you can encourage and praise in the playing.

Parental helping in school

This is an area of school life where you could be tremendously helpful. Where classes are large, demanding activities can only be carried out when extra help is available. Woodwork, knitting, sewing and cooking need an adult's presence all the time, because of the safety factor and the intricacy of the work. Your presence could make all the difference. Parents often have many valuable skills, too, which can enrich children's lives at school

Encouraging creativity at home

Children will be keen to continue various creative activities at home. Make sure that they have the tools they need for creative work and that they know how to use them safely. Don't under-estimate their ability with tools; shown properly, they can be capable and careful. Try setting up a special 'Treasure Chest', containing everything they are likely to need. Then they won't need to keep running to you for bits and pieces and can get to work straight away. They will have plenty of ideas for activities, but don't hesitate to suggest others which occur to you. Join in yourself sometimes, for fun!

A dressing-up box or rail is another source of delight and a tremendous stimulation to drama – you'll learn a great deal about your

This is the ORChestRa and I liked the ORChesrRa and it was in the ofterNoon

by Edward

children (and yourself!) from listening and watching their acting. All they need are:

- old sheets and curtains, cut to manageable lengths;
- old skirts and shirts;
- hats, handbags, shoes and scarves;
- a box of discarded belts;
- a box of old brooches;
- safety pins, tapes and ribbons;
- artificial flowers
- elastic tied in circles, to keep things up.

Museums, galleries and concerts

Museums and galleries have much to offer childen, especially if you go with them, and discuss the exhibits as you go round.

Live music and theatre provide a marvellous experience for children. This is a completely different experience from looking at videos or television. Look out for street theatre and local performances. Schools and churches often put on plays and concerts which young children would love, especially if their older brothers and sisters are performing.

The project

You are certain to have heard your children talk about 'their project'. You may have wondered exactly what this is, why it seems to take up so much time and what the children gain from it. This section sets out to give you some of the answers to your questions. The project can be described as a centre of interest in which many aspects of learning are included. It is an integrated piece of work, involving the use of basic skills and creative work. It is planned to introduce many other subjects not normally taught in their own right at this stage, such as science, history and geography. The starter for the project can come from various sources. However it is started, the teacher must recognise its educational potential before she launches it and decide what she will include. The teacher's

stimulation and direction are absolutely vital. Projects carried out by the children themselves are not suitable at this age, as they are too inexperienced to know what can be derived from any starter, and they do not have the skills to develop the work

What are the advantages of the project?

1 The basic skills of reading, writing and mathematics are used in a way that makes sense to the children and they begin to see how much they need to u these skills as the project unfolds. This gives a point to all their daily efforts.
2 The work is usually of a practical natur and this fits in with our knowledge of how children learn. They will be observing, examining, experimenting, weighing, measuring, counting, etc., a this will in turn lead to recording, charting, drawing, mapping, writing poems and so on. They will learn how find out the answers to relevant questions through experimentation or through reference books; how to set their work out clearly and attractively, and how to choose the best material – fact, they are learning how to organise their work. This will be of enormous us to them in later work, both at school a in outside life.
3 It introduces areas of learning not normally dealt with at infant/first scho stage; their experience of the world is extended and their interests widened. Their interest in the 'subjects' is being stimulated, ready for the time when subject-teaching takes place.
4 Many new facts and a great deal of ne vocabulary is acquired, as the project advances. They are gradually building a store of knowledge about the world.

How is a project carried out?

The project is usually introduced to the whole class by the teacher, who will have prepared her materials beforehand –

pictures, charts, word-lists, reference books, slides, tapes, etc. She will also have organised any outside visits or talks. The actual work can be carried out by:

- the whole class at the same time, each group working on a different aspect of the project;
- in small groups, often of mixed ability, where the more able children can help the slower ones (this is good social training) and each child will make a contribution at the relevant level. Probably, one or two groups will be working at the project whilst the rest are engaged in something else. This makes classroom organisation easier;

- individual children who may continue with their project work when they have completed their work in the basic skills. It is always useful to have something the children can turn to when work is done;
- occasionally, the whole school engages in the same project, each class undertaking an aspect of the work suited to its stage. The finished result is an exciting and impressive display of work, which you are sure to be invited to see.

The diagram below is an example of a project for top infant school children. This project could continue for a whole term as it contains so many aspects of learning.

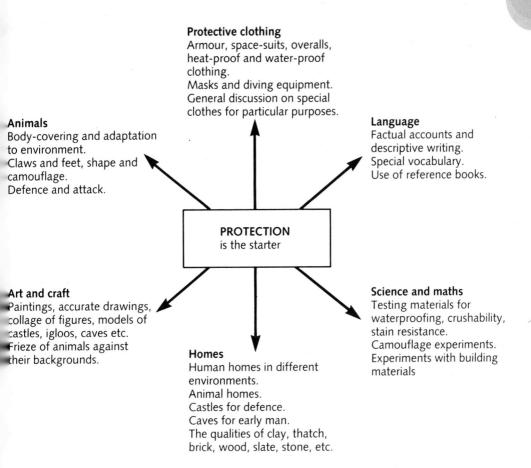

Protective clothing
Armour, space-suits, overalls, heat-proof and water-proof clothing.
Masks and diving equipment.
General discussion on special clothes for particular purposes.

Animals
Body-covering and adaptation to environment.
Claws and feet, shape and camouflage.
Defence and attack.

Language
Factual accounts and descriptive writing.
Special vocabulary.
Use of reference books.

PROTECTION
is the starter

Art and craft
Paintings, accurate drawings, collage of figures, models of castles, igloos, caves etc.
Frieze of animals against their backgrounds.

Science and maths
Testing materials for waterproofing, crushability, stain resistance.
Camouflage experiments.
Experiments with building materials

Homes
Human homes in different environments.
Animal homes.
Castles for defence.
Caves for early man.
The qualities of clay, thatch, brick, wood, slate, stone, etc.

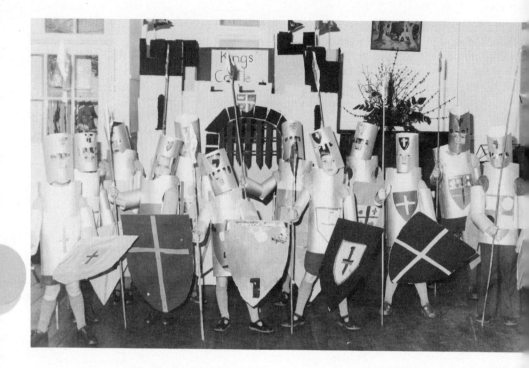

Helping your children in project work

The wider your children's interests are, the more easily they can respond and contribute to the project. So, stimulate their interest with the following:

- Take them on lots of visits, with plenty of discussion – to the zoo, to famous buildings in your area, the local castles, to different towns, to airports and railway stations, to museums and art galleries, to pet shops, factories, farms – everything is grist to the mill of their curiosity.
- Encourage them to ask questions and answer them as fully as you can. If you don't know the answer, look up the facts with the children or find someone who can help you.
- Show them how to look up information for themselves in reference books. All public libraries have reference books in the children's section. Children learn a

great deal from the illustrations, so eve if their reading isn't quite good enough much can be gained.
- Most important of all, show your interest in the school project, and contribute anything towards it which seems relevant.

The above project involved history, language and written work, art and craft, maths (measuring for the armour and castle) and drama. The children presented programme to their parents.

Physical education (PE)

The aims

This is a favourite and very valuable area activity for the children. Its aim is to enab children to develop physically and to acquire control over the movements of the bodies, to gain in self-confidence, daring and stamina; to master the skills needed f games and sports; to learn to cooperate with a group and, later, with a team; to learn to give an immediate response to instructions, (for safety in PE and elsewhere); and, of course, to experience the great pleasure to be derived from physical movement.

However carefully the daily routine is planned, children spend most of their time in the classroom, and they need an opportunity for free, large-scale movement and a release of energy.

What kind of activity will the children meet?

PE in the Hall (or if they are lucky, in a special gymnasium) which is equipped with apparatus, specially designed to stimulate daring movement and to enable the children to stretch, climb, swing, somersault, jump, balance, crawl and twist. In doing this, they are extending their physical skills and exercising all parts of their bodies, in a natural way. The children help to arrange and assemble the apparatus and to clear it away and this requires self-discipline and team-work.

Floor work, where the children space themselves over the floor and movements are practised – skipping, rolling, stretching, galloping etc; starting and stopping at a signal and a good use of space are practised and emphasised.

Work with small apparatus using large and small balls of various kinds, bats, quoits, skipping ropes, hoops, bean-bags and skittles – all these are enjoyed by the children. They may be used quite freely, or a particular skill may be taught. This work will take place outside, when the weather permits.

Games which at this stage mostly involve chasing (usually the teacher!) and a 'home', a signal, and often some chanting, for example, 'Pop goes the weasel' or 'What's the time, Mr Wolf?'. Children must learn to accept the discipline of waiting for the signal before running, of making only for the 'home' and being 'out'. They begin to understand what is meant by 'the luck of the game'.

Dancing/movement to music in which there is tremendous pleasure in moving rhythmically to music and in responding to its mood. This is often provided by the radio lessons which are very imaginatively planned, often presenting sound effects and music of a type no teacher could manage, however skilled. Other types of dancing – folk-dancing, free dancing or miming to music, may be encountered – all of it sets out to promote response to the music, in rhythmic movement and mood.

Swimming, which is organised by most infant/first schools for at least part of the year. Some fortunate schools have their own learner-pool but most use the local baths. It is usually the class-teacher who is in charge. This is comforting for little children, who sometimes find the swimming session rather daunting. At this stage, the aim is to get all children accustomed to the water, to gain confidence so that they can eventually learn to swim. Many attractive aids are used – water-wings, balls, floats, etc. and many young children quickly become good swimmers.

The adventure playground, which many schools are lucky enough to possess. These are often supplied by contributions from parents or money raised by the children themselves. The apparatus may consist of climbing frames, ropes from trees, tyres and bars to swing on, stepping-stones, stockades, balancing walks, a dinghy, large-scale models of cars, space-modules, trains – anything which stimulates imaginative play. Everything is set up outside and classes usually take turns to use it. It is only used when there is a teacher or other responsible adult on duty. It enables the childen to enjoy the type of activities which are natural to them and which are all too often missing, especially in urban environments.

Clothing for PE

For reasons of health and safety, children must strip or change for physical exercise lessons. Extra garments need to be put on when the children begin to cool down after their vigorous activity in the games or PE lesson, to avoid the danger of catching cold. Bare feet can grip the apparatus or floor much more safely than plimsolls. Jumpers, blouses, shirts and long trousers all hamper movement and may catch on the apparatus. So pants and vest, or just pants in the warm weather, are all that are required.

(N.B. All schools are very careful to check floor surfaces for unevenness and splinters and children's feet should be regularly inspected for infection. Anyone who has a foot infection will be excluded from PE, or will do part of the work in plimsolls until the infection has cleared up.)

Please mark all clothing (including shoes) clearly, to ensure the safe return of mislaid articles.

Helping at home and during school

Encourage your children in all forms of exercise. It is a sad reflection of modern times but many young children are overweight and out of condition through lack of sufficient exercise. Young children need to express themselves through physical actions. They often love to dance – provide the music and space for this to be done safely.

Swimming is an important but time-consuming activity. Your help on the journey, in undressing, drying and dressing the children would be much appreciated by the teachers. It helps if you can take your children swimming from time to time yourself – especially in school holidays. Some children (and parents!) become over-anxious about undressing for PE, so see that your child is at least some way towards dressing and undressing him or herself and has acquired the habit of folding and keeping all clothes together in one pile for easy retrieval.

Religious education (RE)

Introduction

The Education Act of 1945 states that all schools should include 'an act of worship' in their day. This is interpreted in many different ways from school to school, according to their circumstances and child-population. Here are some points you might like to consider:

1 Religious beliefs, if held at all, are very personal to the holder, and this makes religious education a difficult matter to discuss. What seems essential to one family may greatly upset another so it is a good idea to consider the general influence and impression on the children rather than becoming too dogmatic.

2 If you hold strong beliefs yourself or if you do not want your children to be influenced by religious ideas at all, find out how RE is dealt with before enrolling them in that school. Although you have the right to withdraw your children from assembly and the scripture lesson, it is always sad for children to be kept out of school happenings.

3 We ought to consider the matter of spiritual and ethical education seriously, both at home and at school. We do tend perhaps to neglect it because, by and large, traditional beliefs are no longer so widely held, and it is a challenging and difficult thing to talk about. But somebody has to accept the responsibility of talking about right and wrong behaviour and about non-materialistic values. At school, assembly is one of the times for this – the quiet atmosphere is right, helped by the music, the poetry, stories and readings and by the united presence of the whole school sharing a moment of stillness together.

4 Most schools consist of children from a

rich variety of backgrounds – black, white, Asians, Europeans, Christians, non-believers, Jews and many more. The children should learn about the Christian religion, especially as so much of our history, traditions and culture have been influenced by it. As we are a multi-racial society, surely they should hear about the other great religions of the world.

Some ways of introducing RE

The Bible-story or RE lesson The story may be chosen from the New or Old Testament and visual aids may be used – pictures, slides, film-strips, videos etc. Or a theme may be chosen and discussed, which is relevant to the children's lives; for example, the care of old people, or helping at home.

Doctrinal teaching This may be given in Church of England, Free Church and Catholic schools. In these schools more emphasis may be placed on RE than in other schools. The day will probably start with an assembly with prayers, hymns and a short talk or Bible-reading. The local vicar, minister or priest will take assembly sometimes and the children will attend church from time to time, especially on the occasion of church festivals.

The assembly The traditional old-fashioned assembly, consisting of a hymn, a prayer, and a few short notices is rare in state schools. Most infant/first school assemblies are delightful and parents are often invited to join in. Modern, tuneful hymns, especially composed and written so that young children can enjoy and understand them, are sung with gusto. Prayers and stories are used which suit the age range. The aim of it all is to foster spiritual awareness in the children. Sometimes, the children will take the assembly themselves, with the help of their teacher, and this is always rather moving.

Assemblies for special religions

Some religions actually forbid children to attend the normal school assembly and where there is a great number of such children in a school, special provision has to be made for them. For example, if there are many Jewish children in the school, the Rabbi might come in to talk to them whilst the main assembly is going on, or, if the number is small, some separate provision must be made for this time.

The most important and influential aspect of spiritual education in school does not depend on the assembly; it derives from the atmosphere which exists in the school. The appreciation of true religious feeling will stem from the way people are treated in the school; on the sympathy shown to those in trouble; on the welcome given to newcomers; on the helping hand extended to those less well-off or handicapped in any way. Tones of voice, the ready smile, the loving attitude – these things will influence your children more positively than all the talk in the world, and these things are what you should look for, and do your part to foster.

The final year

A summing up

The first years of school pass so quickly: before you know where you are, your children will be in their final year and you will be beginning to think of the next stage in their education. They will have made enormous progress in these years, in maturation as well as in work, and their importance cannot be over-estimated, since this is the time when the foundations of learning take place. During the last year, the basic skills are revised and tidied up and all aspects of work are pulled together. Sometimes, especially in first schools, a little subject teaching is introduced to prepare for this in the junior school. It is comforting to know that much of what the children have learnt in the infant/first school, will be revised again at junior level, and the children will be able to continue at their own stage of work, as far as is possible.

What will they have gained?

- They will have made a good start in mastering the basic skills of reading, writing, spelling and sentence construction. They will understand and be able to work with the number system, and will have had a wide range of mathematical experiences.
- They will have had practical experiences of all kinds, be able to select the relevant equipment for a task, and use tools safely and efficiently. They will be able to set about solving a simple problem and to record their findings in many ways. They will have learnt how to use books for reference.
- They will have experienced the pleasure of creative work and may have developed skills in a particular aspect of this.
- They will have gained in physical skills and control, daring and stamina.
- They will have learnt how to work – perhaps the most important thing of all – and how to organise themselves and their equipment. They will have improved their ability to listen, concentrate, become involved and settle quietly to work, often without any reference to the teacher.

- They will have developed some social graces – the ability to work with others and share the teacher's attention; the ability to make friends with some people and tolerate others. They will understand what is meant by a community and be able to fit into the school unit.
- They will have developed a positive attitude towards school and the activities it introduces, and be in a better position to tackle new experiences.

These are tremendous gains and there are many more, too numerous to mention. You will not, of course, expect all children to have achieved all this; progress, as always, must depend on the child and there are bound to be wide differences.

Looking ahead

Most children of this age are ready for the wider world and larger community of the junior school. They may be moving on with a group of friends and, in the case of a combined infants and junior school, to a familar community. In these combined schools, the children's education often flows smoothly on with few changes. In most junior schools, the educational philosophy is very similar to that of infant and first schools so when discussing the next stage of the children's school life I shall highlight only those aspcts which may be different.

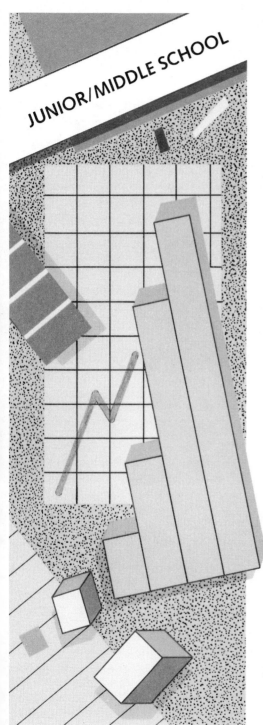

JUNIOR/MIDDLE SCHOOL

Introduction

Children at this stage – between the ages of 7 to 11 or 12 years – are enthusiastic, receptive and full of fun and energy. As they are on the way towards a competent use of the basic skills their work can be extended and taken to greater depths.

There are many similarities between infant/first schools and junior/middle schools. In the first year or two, the same child-centred approach may be seen, with its emphasis on practical work, group-work and integration of subjects. The staffing situation is also likely to be much the same. There may be more specialisation as the skills of the children in some areas of the curriculum increase, for example, in science or music. There may be more male teachers on the staff (masters are rare in infant/first schools, unfortunately). Towards the middle of the school, you will probably find more class and subject teaching, indeed, some junior schools and many middle schools start this straight away. This cuts across the practice of having one teacher responsible for one class and remaining with them throughout the day, thereby building a close relationship with the children. There are points in favour of both approaches; the most usual solution is to keep to the general class-teacher for the first year to two, changing to specialist teaching thereafter. This gives the school a chance to assess the abilities of the children, who have been gathered from many different schools and backgrounds, and to start off with a thorough revision of the basic skills. It also provides a stable environment for the children, as they settle into their new school.

Choosing the school

Choosing a junior school is not such a problem as choosing an infant school, as most children tend to move on to the local school with their friends. You can, of course, change schools at this stage. It is easier perhaps for you to consider more distant schools, as your children are somewhat older and can manage the journey better. However, do bear in mind that in junior schools there may be after-school activities which your children will not want to miss. This extension of the day should be taken into account before making a decision.

Admission is simple at this stage, too. All the children start on the same day, and at the same time, as a rule. First and middle schools usually have a very close link; they are often in the same building, so moving from one to the other is easy.

Traditional or progressive?

Are you perplexed about the differences between these types of schools? A 'traditional' school is often thought of as one in which class and subject teaching predominate, with little attempt to reach the different ability levels of the children. We visualise desks/tables formally arranged in rows; and the teaching mainly 'chalk and talk'. Text books and small exercise books are much in use and there is little opportunity for practical work. A 'progressive' school we think of as providing child-centred education, with much practical work and group teaching, of animated classrooms with some movement and conversation, much discussion from the teacher and an integration of subjects.

Most schools do not fall into either one or the other of these categories but use a mixture of both methods of teaching, for both have advantages. Most primary schools try to match their teaching to each child's stage of learning and therefore teach in groups. Class-teaching is used for a specific purpose, e.g. setting a piece of work in which all childen are to be involved, or in religious education or history. Then, they will expect the class to listen with concentration. You can find good and bad

schools of both persuasions. As with everything connected with school, the excellence of the school depends upon the commitment and expertise of the staff.

Visiting the junior/middle school

You may have made a link already with your junior/middle school. You may have visited it with your childen or had an appointment for registration arranged for you. If not, visit the schools in which you are interested before committing your child to any one. When you are looking round the school, the same criteria hold good as for infant/first schools. Try to assess the general atmosphere, relationships, organisation, work-standards and discipline, in the same way as you did before.

Questions to think about Many will be the same as those you asked previously, but some will relate specifically to the junior/middle school:

- Where do most of the children go on to from here? This may not loom very large at the moment but is important to know what your options are likely to be later.
- Is the integrated work of the infant stage continued and for how long? When is subject teaching introduced? Are the children taught formally for any part of the day?
- Is homework set? If so, when, and how much?
- How are parents informed about progress in work? Are tests held? Are school records kept? Are end-of-term reports sent home? Are there open days/evenings?
- Are there after-school activities, outings clubs, school holidays, etc?
- Are games played? Are there swimming sport activities and athletics, etc?
- Is individual tuition in music given and are instruments on loan at first? Is there a school orchestra?

The main changes for the children

The worries about junior school life are reduced for children because, by now, they understand what a school community is like. If they feel apprehensive at all, it is because anything new is slightly alarming.

Here are the main changes that may cause some apprehension:

1 The community is likely to be larger and will contain many new faces. There will be children from different backgrounds and some difficult children, who can make life worrying.
2 They may be worried about their work, especially if they have had problems before. The extension, however, will come gradually and as they are ready for it. This stretching is an important part of junior school life.
3 The school day is slightly longer and work periods may be extended.
4 There will be interaction with many more teachers. Some children find this confusing at first, and feel lost. Although your children may miss the cosiness of the infant school to start with, they will come to enjoy this diversity.

These worries are likely to resolve themselves, as the children become accustomed to the new routines. If there are areas of the work which cause persistent anxiety, encourage them to ask for help. Children of this age should feel confident enough to do this. A session with the teacher at playtime or after school can usually put things right. If your children won't approach the teacher, try to sort things out yourself; failing that, visit the classroom to get help. But don't be in too much of a hurry to do this; it is better that they manage for themselves.

Preparing for the first day of term

- Talk to your children about the differences between junior and infant school. Point out its greater opportunities and demands. Prepare them for the mass of children, the number of staff, the movement from place to place throughout the day, the stricter discipline, and so on. You may have met the class-teacher, or at least been given a name; use this, and discuss the potential pleasures of the class.
- During the long summer holidays make sure that some reading and writing are done and that spelling, tables and number facts are kept up to scratch. Children do forget during these long breaks and a little polishing up will make sure that your children start the new school with confidence.
- Make sure you have all the equipment needed for school and that all clothing is clearly marked.
- Arrive at school well on time, but not over-early – a long wait in the playground is best avoided on the first day. Link them up with a friend or two.

The evening after

You would be forgiven if you go to meet your children for the first week or two, though be prepared for them to resist this after a while. You should continue to meet them if the journey home is dangerous in any way, despite their protests. You will be longing to hear all about the new venture but let the children tell you as much or as little as they wish; they will be tired and bemused and it will take time for them to sort it all out. Organise a calm evening with some outside activity if possible. They have been indoors for most of the day and this comes hard to energetic youngsters.

Home back-up

Now that your children can manage life on their own, at least in some aspects, it is tempting to think that they are off your hands. In some ways they are but they still need to feel your support, though this may be expressed in a different way. Their growing independence must be recognised and encouraged, but they must be sure of your interest and affection. They need to know that they are important family members. You can help them to mature into reliable people by making them responsible for some aspect of daily life such as setting and clearing the table or doing a little shopping. Show that you trust them by letting them get on with it on their own and give praise if the result is satisfactory. Don't hesitate to criticise if this is needed; they usually know perfectly well when the job is slipshod so don't let it pass.

It is a good idea to continue to give your junior school children a special time with you, without the others, when your attention is focused solely on them. These times are important to them, and to you, and it is worth foregoing another activity to enable this to take place. Children at this stage respond to being treated in quite a grown-up fashion. The attitudes and relationships you establish now will influence they way they respond to you later!

Homework

Most primary schools do not set regular homework (though middle schools may) but most schools do send home reading books to practise, tables to learn, spellings to consolidate and work to finish off. They also often ask children to find out information at home for the project. If your children are given any work to do, set aside a time for it – after tea perhaps, when they have had a break from school. If you take the homework seriously, so will the children; if you push it aside as a nuisance, so will they. Try to continue with your support with learning by heart – they will appreciate it if you test them. It is helpful if there is any encyclopedia, an atlas and a dictionary at home for the children to use.

At first, children love to do homework because it makes them feel grown-up; but if it is set regularly there may come a time when it palls. This is where your interest and involvement will pay dividends. It is not a good idea to let the homework become a constant source of worry, causing a nightly trauma for everyone. Have a word with the teacher if this is the case, and find out the cause for the reluctance. It could be lack of understanding or stem from a run-down condition. It may stem from idleness, in which case you will have to present a firm front.

Parental help in school

This is usually very welcome in junior/middle schools, especially during the first year or two when group work and integrated learning are likely to be followed. Ask the Head or Deputy Head about this; they will arrange with you the best time to visit and how your help should be used. There is no better way of gaining an understanding of teaching methods and school practices and of the difficulties and pleasure of teaching, than to help with the work in school. You have the opportunity to get to know the teachers as people and they will cease thinking of you in an anonymous way as 'parents'.

Some initial worries for parents

Sometimes, with the change-over from the small protective infant school to the more challenging junior school, a few problems arise. These usually vanish after a period of adjustment but let's have a look at some of the common ones:

An apparent regression in the work

During the first term or two, the teacher will be engaged in discovering the work standards of the new group of children and in revising. The new class probably consists of children from many schools and with differing backgrounds and abilities. Even though records passed on from the previous school will give some idea of work covered, methods will vary and practices will be forgotten. No school is going to sort its children into working sets until this basic revision has been done. Your children may well be meeting work that is easy for them, for a short while. This does not matter; it will engender confidence in a new situation. Do not worry about this unless it continues for too long and your child loses interest; in which case, a word with the class-teacher or Headteacher is indicated.

Different methods and expectations

Your children may well meet these and must learn to accept them. Each school has its own way of doing things and its own expectations. One school will allow the children to walk in noisily from play; another will expect them to stand still at the bell, line up, and walk in formally. One school will insist on the date for every piece of work; another will not make an issue of it. You can help by discussing this with your children and comparing homes with different expectations. Children soon learn what is wanted and come to accept it.

Lapses in behaviour

A marked change in behaviour, manners and speech sometimes occurs at the start of junior school. This often worries parents as their lovely children appear to change before their very eyes. It happens when the children meet different modes of behaviour and different types of speech, especially if most of their school-mates adopt these habits. Children hate to be different from the mass, and are very imitative. The best method of dealing with speech and vocabulary anomolies is to ignore them completely, without apparent shock or

upset. Make sure they are not hearing the very words you are objecting to in the home or on television. If this is the case you must not be surprised if they repeat them with gusto.

Children sometimes use rough speech and swear words for effect, either to impress their mates or to draw attention to themselves in moments of stress at home. Stand firm in your decision about the dispute in hand, ignoring the broadsides, which will probably peter out. If you express great shock, this weapon will surely be used again. Choose a nice, calm moment to talk about this with them. As far as behaviour and attitudes to others are concerned, you would be right to insist on your own established codes of behaviour at home. Reasons for these can be discussed but adhere firmly to these standards. Children will accept the idea that what passes in the school playground will not necessarily pass at home. They need to feel that framework there if they are to feel secure.

Children who don't settle

Sometimes children who have been very happy and successful at infant school are far from happy at junior school. They seem to take an unreasonably long time to settle. When you try to find out the trouble you get a string of complaints – the playground is too rough, or the teacher shouts, or it's too noisy at dinner-time, or they haven't got any friends, and so on. None of these circumstances seem to bother other children and naturally, you are worried. Check up first that friends do exist and cement any friendships by an invitation to tea, or to join an outing at the weekend. Children's friendships at this stage are rather fickle. Maybe, with all the choice of new friends, your children have temporarily been abandoned. After this you can only give it time. Some children do take a very long time to adapt to changes. If you continue to feel anxious, discuss the problem with the class-teacher. You will get the inside view of your child's school behaviour and find out how he or she is mixing with others. Maybe the child is rejecting advances or is slightly aggressive. Maybe there has been some bullying in the playground, which can be dealt with. If you share the problem you can usually find a solution.

Finding out about progress

There is usually less daily contact between the staff and parents at junior school than there was in the infant school. There is not the same need for this now that the children are growing in independence. It may be that you will not find the same opportunities for informal talks as before. How do you find out about the children's progress.? There are several ways and here are some of them, though these vary from school to school.

The open evening

These are occasions when parents are invited to school to discuss their children's work. They are held after school or in the evening so that parents can attend, without the presence of their children if possible. You may be allowed to bring the children with you if you have no-one with whom to leave them, but do not expect the discussion to take place with them at your side – teachers do not like discussing children in their hearing. All aspects of the work – the workbooks, social attitudes, classroom behaviour and standards – can come under scrutiny. These talks are very helpful to the staff in their daily interaction with your children. If the school is large, separate evenings may be arranged for each year group and a timed appointment is given to each family. Although you need plenty of time for discussion you have to remember that there are many parents coming after you and the evening is not

endless. So if you have a point to discuss that you know will take a very long time, make a separate appointment for another time.

The yearly/termly report

This is a more formalised progress report and is not very detailed. It is usually a summing-up of the year or term's work. It will give you some idea of where the strengths and weaknesses of your child lie, with a general comment on behaviour, attitudes, involvement and commitment to school life.

The talk with the teacher

Teachers at junior school are always glad to discuss your children's progress with you where there is a real need. In most cases, this can be left to the official times. However, if you are really concerned, don' sit at home worrying or pestering your children with questions they cannot answer. Make an appointment with the Head, giving the reason for your request. The longer children are left to flounder, the harder it is to put the matter right.

The evening meeting

These often give information about a particular area of the curriculum and provide a chance for teachers to explain methods and objectives, as well as for you to ask questions. Their main function is to help you to understand what is going on i school, so that you can follow your children's work better.

The open day

The whole school is opened up to the parents and interested outsiders and you are invited to walk round the school and se teaching taking place. This is not the time t ask about your children's work – the staff will be much too busy. It provides an opportunity to see the school in action an both parents and children enjoy it.

Examinations and tests

Most primary schools only set informal classroom tests but these are usually diagnostic, not competitive. National tests for young children may be imposed by the government in the near future. Whatever the exam or test, the practice of grading the children from top to bottom only confirms the brilliance of a few and depresses the rest. It is better to encourage the children to compare their own results – 'Did you do better than last time?' is the vital question. This does not mean that excellence is not striven after but it does mean that all children can receive their share of praise for effort expended and work well done. It is beneficial for all children to see the outstanding work of the brilliant few – it shows what can be done; but it is senseless and cruel to compare this with work from average or slow children, thereby instilling them with a damaging sense of failure. The brilliant children must also learn to judge the work of others in this way, or a horrid conceit will develop. Children are very quick to recognise those who are clever, or wonderful at PE, or gifted musically. They know, too, who are the slow ones and who are the class nuisances. They don't need examination results to confirm this. Teachers know these things too – it is their job to do so and they will inform you where your child stands in comparison with the rest, if you feel you want to know and have not already sensed this. It is wise to accept the teacher's opinion, since she is in a position to compare abilities, not only with the present class but also with children previously taught.

Most schools test the children's reading at least once a year. Some tests are of a general nature, some are geared more to comprehension, while others are diagnostic i.e. they pinpoint areas where the children find special difficulty. Some tests give the children a 'reading age'; this compares their performance with the average for their age,

for example, a child with severe reading problems may have a reading age well below the actual age, whilst a child who is reading well will come out above the actual age. Many children have reading ages above their chronological age. Most schools test mathematical progress too.

Discipline in the junior school

The discipline established in the junior school will be based on:

- the need to ensure the safety of the children;
- the need to maintain an atmosphere in which learning can take place;
- the need to ensure happy social relationships within the school.

It is of the utmost importance to your children that you support the school over matters of discipline. So first make sure you know what is expected of them and if anything is absolutely forbidden. If punishment is needed, it will not be in the form of physical chastisement but will consist of a withdrawal of privileges or a removal from the scene of the crime – usually the classroom or the playground – to spend time in the Head's room, working. The Head, Deputy Head or class-teacher – or all three – will talk the problem through with the children. You may be called in to add your voice to the discussion. This is no soft option but very formidable indeed. Other children often exert pressure on those who bully or upset others. In the classroom, the teacher must take a firm stand against constant chatter during working periods, arguing or fighting in class, refusal to get on with work, rudeness, or the deliberate interference with other children. These forms of behaviour can ruin the working atmosphere and prevent the teacher from carrying out the proper function of teaching.

71

If you sense that your child is causing trouble in class, do tackle it head-on. Make sure that they understand that you will have none of it and join forces with the teacher, backing up any decision that is taken. Return to school from time to time (and let your children know you plan to do this) to see that all is well and to show that you are keeping an eye on things. You could reward them, too, if they have made an effort to toe the line.

Occasionally, the discipline of the whole class is poor, leading to bad behaviour generally. Children will play up if the chance is there. Many parents may worry about this with good reason. This is a matter for the Head, who will almost certainly be aware of the situation already. The cause may be a young teacher in need of some extra help and support; or it may be a teacher who does not motivate the children sufficiently, with resulting boredom leading to naughtiness. It may be a small group of very disruptive children in the class, or even one severely disturbed child. Whatever the cause, the Head will deal with it. In the very rare cases where nothing seems to improve, you can take the matter further and get in touch with the school governors, who will ensure that something is done. But this is a last resort; it is always better for any problem to be dealt with inside the school by the Head, who is in the strongest position to do this.

Staff and parents as partners

Please do

- back up the school with your support, whenever you can;
- participate fully in the PTA or other parent-school organisation;
- help in the work inside the school;
- find out about teaching methods and school discipline;
- keep a sense of proportion over the annoying things which are bound to happen sometimes – the paint-spotted shirt, the lost shoe, the torn belt or the 'telling-off'; you could do without these irritations, but consider the crowded classroom and playground. Teachers do develop eyes at the back of their heads but, even so, cannot control everyone all the time;
- see that articles which have 'strayed' home and do not belong to your children are returned to school, preferably by the children. Trouble later on often starts with very small incidents and you can help set standards from the very beginning for your children.

Please don't

- compare your children's progress with that of others, especially other members of the family. Compare each child with his or her own standard and try to find something for which you can give praise first before you start to criticise.
- grumble with other parents at the school gate, forming a little clique; this generates ill-feeling and is not very useful. Get it off your chest at home when the children are not there. Then come and talk to the school about the matter.

In all things, consider the Head and staff as your partners in the education of your children. Teaching is a rewarding but sometimes disheartening work. The teachers are doing their best to fulfil your expectations and to satisfy their own. They need and deserve your support in this demanding and vital task.

School and classroom organisation

Most junior/middle school children are grouped in mixed ability classes. In order to teach all the subjects efficiently, ability groups may be formed, especially in the basic skills. Other subjects will either be covered by the project or taken as class lessons; here, the teacher will expect the resulting work to reach different standards, according to each child's ability.

Some junior/middle schools introduce subject teaching in class lessons straight away. Some leave this until the upper end of the school, believing this gives sufficient time for the children to become accustomed to subject teaching before leaving school.

Middle schools may set their children into ability groups for some subjects; this means drawing together all children of a similar ability from the various classes. Middle schools are likely to have more specialist teachers in subjects such as maths, science and languages; this will influence their organisation.

Work in the junior/middle school

Language work

Reading

There is much necessary overlap with the infant/first school in the teaching of reading because children must progress according to their own stage. Graded readers and reading schemes are used until the children become fluent, that is, can read well any book they are likely to meet. Records are kept of their attainment and if it is necessary, remedial help can be given. It is important that the reading books presented to children should, as far as possible, match their interests and age. Infant readers are to be avoided since the children with problems would feel down-graded by these. Reading is practised in various ways:

- silent reading for pleasure, with a free choice of books;
- in pairs, or groups, where one child can help another;
- through a reading scheme where this is still needed. Here, the children are frequently heard by the teacher or other adult;
- class reading, where everyone reads (or tries to read) the same book, either in turn, or following the teacher. This often takes place in history and geography.

Parental involvement in reading A very exciting recent development in the teaching of reading is the involvement of parents, both at school and in the home. It has been proved by surveys that children whose parents are working with the school in this way do much better even than children given remedial help at school. Try to get involved with this if you can, especially if your children are having difficulties. The teacher will supply the books and other materials needed and will show you exactly what to do. You work with your own children, in school or at home, and a real partnership will be established between you, your children and the teacher.

Reading for comprehension
Comprehension in reading assumes great importance – there is not much point in reading, if the words and content are not understood. As subject teaching develops, textbooks are used to give information – and understanding is vital. Teachers often find that though children can decipher the actual words, they have little idea of the meaning. So emphasis is placed on this at junior level and special textbooks, containing passages with questions, are used for this purpose. Children are questioned on their individual reading books, too, and may be asked to write a short account of the plot or give an opinion on it.

Books in the school and at home There should be a good selection of books, both in the classroom and in the school library. Many schools take advantage of the Schools' Library Service which enables them

The school library. Children love browsing through books, especially if these are well displayed.

to borrow a large selection of books every term. Encourage your children to use the school library and make sure that they belong to the local library too. Help them to build up a library of their own; second-hand book shops, fairs and jumble sales are all sources of supply for books.

Vocabulary extension

There are many opportunities for this at junior level with the introduction of new subjects, each with their special vocabulary. Through reading, through discussion, through science, history, geography and enviromental studies, to say nothing of computer studies, children are not only meeting new words but also learning how to use them.

Handwriting

A particular style is likely to be adopted throughout the school and practice is necessary to obtain a good result. Children

are required to write a great deal more, an at greater speed, in the junior school, so th sooner they are able to master this skill, th better. Joined handwriting is introduced a the right time; this is when the print letter are formed clearly and correctly. This even is one of the major thrills of junior school life. Ink is not used until the upper end of the school, when cartridge pens are advocated as a rule. When your children reach this stage, it is wise to see that they are equipped with a spare cartridge or tw for emergencies and that their precious pens are marked with their name. Sticky tape will keep the name tag round the pe barrel.

Spelling

Phonic and irregular words are revised an new spelling rules are taught. There is mu to learn:

- related and rhyming words;
- tricky words;

- many-syllabled words;
- confusing words e.g. sight and site, wear, where and were.

You will have sympathy for young children as they struggle with the irregularities of the English language. Children with a strong visual sense, who notice small differences, are often good spellers; others have to learn by rote or by using the sounds. Children use a dictionary at this stage and there are likely to be word lists available to them, for help.

The English lesson

All the work discussed so far will be practised in the English lesson and the skills will be used throughout the day in all other subjects. Vocabulary work, spelling, punctuation, sentence-construction and comprehension will be consolidated by the use of attractive textbooks. This work on words is popular and helps children to focus their attention on details. It is relatively easy to achieve success, too, so it encourages those with problems. It is reasonable to expect children to produce written work containing content and ideas, legibly written in clear sentences, properly punctuated and with satisfactory spelling, by the age of 10 or 11 years.

The real test of all written English work is the content, and how well this is expressed. Many children write well at this stage, producing poems with original ideas, cleverly planned stories and logical accounts with real factual content.

Mathematics

The maths scheme

Junior/middle school mathematics usually follows a maths scheme, which may be planned by the Headteacher or the Head of Maths, together with the staff. Suggestions from the local authority Advisor for Primary Maths may well form the foundation for discussion. The scheme is structured to

> ### Urban Snow
>
> Hazy figures are no longer visible,
> They merge into the dull greys and
> Browns of the city shops and the ground.
>
> Snow falls, and then dissolves
> On the pavement, because the ground is too
> Wet for it to settle.
>
> Little children slip and slide on the
> slushy ground, Mothers curse it and
> Sooth their offspring.
>
> Business men ruin their overcoats and
> Are not pleased with this
> Sudden change of the weather.
>
> But in spite of these accusations, the
> Snow still falls, never giving in.
> Never tiring.
>
> At twelve o'clock the people return to
> Their homes for lunch. Only the shoveller
> Remains, continuing his melancholy job.

Rowena – aged 10.

ensure all the necessary work in maths is covered at the proper stages as the children progress through the school. The scheme is usually accompanied by attractive textbooks, which contain both suggestions and guidance for practical work and introduce the relevant mathematical language and symbols. The textbooks will also provide practice and revision in all areas of the work including traditional 'sums'. There may be sections for tables, number facts, notation and other basic work, to give extra practice. Workcards are likely to be used to supplement the textbooks, and many teachers make their own, to suit individual children.

In the junior or middle school it is probable that the whole class will work at maths at the same time – and they will do so every day. Children usually enjoy maths. It is very important for the teacher to keep up this enthusiasm and to make absolutely certain that the children realise that this subject is concerned with real situations in the real world and does not consist merely of pages of sums in exercise books. Practical work demonstrates this to them and, moreover, shows them why tables and sums are an essential part of the work.

The work covered

You will be astonished at the variety of work your children will be learning as they progress through the school. Here are some of the maths introduced:

- the 24-hour clock; time; time-tables and calendars;
- problems on time, distance and speed;
- statistics and graphical representation;
- calculations in numbers, decimals, fractions and money;
- percentages and ratios;
- maps, scales and grids;
- algebraical equations and problem-solving;
- symmetry and tessellation;
- measurement and weight;
- areas and volumes;
- geometry – angles, properties of shapes, special triangles, etc;
- pie-charts and Venn diagrams;
- sets, sub-sets, attributes of members, partitioning etc;
- properties of numbers: square numbers, prime numbers, cube numbers, square roots, lowest common factors, factors, multiples;
- calculations on bases other than 10
- all multiplication tables up to 10; multiplying by 20, by 100, and the converse, division.

All of this work relies on a real understanding of numbers, a knowledge of tables and a complete grasp of the system of notation. It will be accompanied by practical work and discussion, after which it will be recorded.

Notation Notation, or the understanding

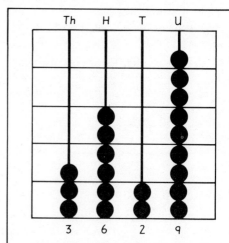

Three thousand, six hundred and twenty-nine.

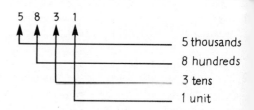

5 thousands
8 hundreds
3 tens
1 unit

of place values, is a vital part of mathematics. Here are a few of the ways this is reinforced:

1 Make the biggest possible number, using all these figures: 4, 1, 9, 5
   9, 541
   nine thousand, five hundred and forty one

2 Now make the smallest:
   1, 459
   one thousand, four hundred and fifty nine

3 What is the biggest figure you can have in any column? 9

4 What is the value of the underlined figure?
   4 286 . . . 2 hundreds
   1 302 . . . 0 tens

5 How many whole tens are there in this number?
   974   97 tens

and this
1230   123 tens

Work in a real situation – open-ended maths

Open-ended maths can be described as work which could go in any direction and can be taken to any lengths. This requires very clear thought and the use of many kinds of 'sums'. Here is an example:

A boy may be asked to find out how long it would take him to walk to the next town or village or any place within reasonable distance. He will not be told how to tackle this problem, though it may be discussed with the teacher and other children first. He must think out his own method.

1 He will measure a distance of 50 metres in the playground, using a metre trundle wheel or, if this is lacking, two metre sticks and chalk.
2 He will walk this distance, while a friend times him with the stopwatch. Let us suppose it takes him 4 minutes. He will then work out:
     50 metres takes 4 minutes
     100 metres will take 8 minutes
     1000 metres, or 1 kilometre, will take 80 minutes = 1 hr 20 min.
3 With the use of an ordnance survey or town map, he will measure the required distance, using string, which will go round the twists and turns. He will straighten out the string and measure it.
4 He will look at the scale of the map: it is 2 centimetres to 1 kilometre. The string measures 5 cm so the real distance is 2½ km.
5 He will work out that 1 km takes him 1 hour 20 min to walk
    2½ km will take 2½ x 1 hour 20 min
    = 2 hrs 40 min + 40 min
    = 3 hrs 20 min.

A variety of mathematical thinking is involved in this work and the boy himself must decide how to tackle it. Children will be able to cope with demanding work of this nature if they have had plenty of practical experience with real things in real situations.

Mathematical problems

These are real situations expressed in words only. The open-ended work above is really a 'problem', with the boy actually doing it. If this boy met a similar problem in an examination paper he would know how to do it because of his previous work. If children have handled materials, weighed, measured, filled containers, and so on, when they are young, they will probably find problems easy and fun. It is those children who are taught 'sums' by rote who cannot decide what is required of them.

Project work and subject-teaching

The project versus history, geography and science

Each school will decide on whether these areas of the curriculum will be taught separately as subjects in their own right or should continue to be integrated with the project. Some schools may manage to fit in both subject-teaching and the project. The teachers understand well the value of this, yet feel that at this stage there is the need for a more structured approach in these areas. There is a need to draw together the knowledge the children have gained so far in their project-work. In the hands of an experienced and enthusiastic teacher, nothing can be more exciting than subject-teaching and this provides the opportunity to check that the basic core of the subject is taught and some idea of the logical sequence of events is given. Children enjoy learning in this new way but care must be taken to see that the practical work connected with the subject is not overlooked; this is especially true of geography, environmental studies and most of all with science.

The project

This will be taken to a much greater depth than at infant level and more areas of learning are included. Children will be encouraged to discover their own sources of information, both in school and outside. By now, children understand what is meant by a project and are often set to plan their own work, choosing a topic which interests them. This provides a good opportunity for them to use their skills of reading, writing, mathematics and artwork to some purpose as well as thinking about the organisation of the work. One of the main functions of the project is to widen children's horizons and stimulate fresh enthusiasms, so the child-orientated project should not be the only kind they meet.

In the junior school, the project may be chosen for its actual 'learning' potential. This flow-chart gives some suggestions for

Mathematics
Looking at scales on the map.
Practice in scale-work.
Times of journeys – then and now.
Size of ships.
Fathoms

Art and craft
Paintings of voyages.
Models of ships.
A classroom frieze of all explorers in chronological order with related pictures.

Language
Imaginary stories of voyages.
Accounts of true explorations
Use of reference books.
Poems about the sea, storms, lone voyages, strange lands.

EXPLORATION AND DISCOVERY

Science
Experiments on floating and sinking.
Experimenting with magnets.
Investigating streamlining.
Making a compass with a magnestised needle.

History
Stories of selected explorers with their historical backgrounds.
Quiz game – who discovered what?
Exploration in space.

Geography
Map-work.
Becoming familiar with continents and oceans.
Use of a compass for finding direction, some orienteering.
Geographical terms.
Map tracing.
Finding routes.

a project on Exploration and Discovery, perhaps started off by a TV programme. Visits to a suitable museum or exhibition will be planned, and slides/videos/films arranged.

A mass of stimulating work could emerge from such a starter. The children will be using their basic skills in very demanding situations and acquiring some new ones, too. Their vocabulary will have been extended by the specialist words used and they will have learnt many facts about an interesting subject.

History

Local history is usually emphasised more than world history, and social more than political events, though these may be used as a peg on which to hang more general work. The history of the locality; the way people lived in the past; their houses, clothes, food, occupations, beliefs and life-styles – these provide an interesting start to the study of history. Some schools take significant events as starters for their work - the Crusades, the Norman invasion, the Vikings, the great explorers, the opening up of America, or any subject which may arise from television or a local exhibition. Whatever the opening, history is a popular subject with children providing it is made relevant to them. The work is often recorded and illustrated in a special notebook and exciting models are made. Attractively illustrated textbooks are used to provide background information and the reference books in the library will be in great demand.

Geography and environmental studies

These subjects, too, usually stem from the locality first. Exciting fieldwork can take place. This may include examining weather conditions, looking at soil samples, collecting different types of rock, or examining local rivers and parks, and looking at the materials used for building—

A project on castles at Junior level. At this stage, the work is more detailed, and the models more precise.

Children enjoy looking at maps and the globe, especially if there is someone to discuss it with.

79

anything relevant is pressed into service. Children at this age love maps and globes and should be beginning to acquire a knowledge of the world, its countries and climates, especially as we see so much of distant places on television. Foreign countries are all part of our lives now and children should know where these places are and what is the difference between a country and a county, a capital city and a town. Textbooks will be selected according to the scheme in the school. The work will possibly be recorded in a large-scale book, as maps, diagrams etc. take up so much space.

History and geography are often integrated – indeed, it is sometimes difficult to know where one stops and the other starts. This is particularly the case when the locality is being studied.

Science

Science is enormously popular with children because it is active and about real things. It is becoming increasingly important in the primary school curriculum because it provides opportunities for logical thinking and problem-solving and, although it is often included in projects, it needs to be taught in its own right. At this stage we are not concerned with the traditional image of science – the laboratories, the bunsen burner, the chemicals and the test-tube – we are concerned with encouraging children to:

- become ever more curious about the world, and to ask relevant questions;
- to invent and carry out simple experiments to enable them to answer these questions;
- to be critical of their results and to be able to consider factors which may affect these results;
- to learn about the properties of materials – soil, water, sand, rock, air, paper, wood and so on;

Looking at snails. Careful observation is an important part of science.

80

Working with a Speaking tube

We experimented with a speaking tube. We found out whispering sounded louder through the tube. This was because the sound was closed in.

Greg   7 years

to touch on subjects such as magnetism, electricity, sound and heat;
to learn about plant and animal life and its interdependence;
to learn about ecology and conservation;
to be able to organise and record their work in all this clearly and logically.

The work is usually launched through an umbrella title, such as:

Sound
Animals in their environment
Time
Magnetism
Sight and Hearing
Hedge study
Movement

The work will explore different aspects of the subject and close observation, experimentation, recording and critical analysis will be an important part of it all. Textbooks may be used to give a structure and as a source of information, but the vital part of the work is practical. It is bound to include much mathematics and language work, providing a marvellous opportunity for discussion and the introduction of new vocabulary.

Creative work

Introduction

Parents do sometimes wonder whether too much time is spent on creative work. They consider it as a pleasant extra and not really essential to the children's learning. Schools are concerned with the education of the whole child. We want an education which will help children to mature into confident, stable adults, able to take their place in a life enriched by all aspects of their education. This is why creative work is seen as an essential part of your children's school life.

We have already discussed how children are likely to benefit from creative work, in the infant section. All children need the emotional release and satisfaction these activities bring, especially as at this stage, school work is generally more demanding. The skills they master will enable them to become more self-sufficient in coping with their daily life.

Art and craft

During junior/middle school life your children gain greater control over their tools and their work will become more complex. They will be encouraged to look at colours, shapes, textures and patterns more closely. Although they will sometimes be given free

This little girl is enjoying using her increased skills in making a doll.

choice of subject and materials, the teacher may also make suggestions to focus their attention on a particular aspect of the work – a pattern made up of curves only; a painting in greys, whites, blues and blacks. New skills and techniques will be introduced for there has to be progress in art, as in all other subjects and for this, teaching and discussion are necessary. Model-making will become more sophisticated, as children demand greater realism and crafts such as weaving, basketry, wood-carving, pottery, tie-dye work, tapestry, printing and sewing may be offered to boys and girls alike.

Cookery

In middle schools there is often a special room for domestic science with cookery as a regular part of the syllabus. In junior schools, cookery will take place from time to time, or in a regular rota. You may be asked to supply the ingredients and possibly the cake tins, when your child's turn comes along. Parents often come into school to help supervise the cookery group and to share their expertise.

Music

This really takes off in the junior/middle school. The musical education and experiences available in some primary schools is outstanding. It does depend sadly on the presence of either a visiting specialist or on a gifted teacher within the school. Television and radio programmes, tapes and records and percussion instruments and possibly recorders, are used in schools to give the children the chance to make music themselves. Your children may have the experience of:

- class singing and the school choir;
- recorder playing, as individuals and perhaps as an ensemble. The recorder is a good instrument to start children off on their musical journey; it is easy to handle, fairly inexpensive and they produce results quite quickly;

...he brass band. Playing together is one of the highlights of music-making.

percussion playing which, if treated seriously as a musical form, can achieve a really high standard of excellence at this stage, especially if it is combined with voices, recorders and other instruments;
individual tuition in instrumental playing – violin, cello, trumpet, guitar, piano and many others – which leads to the marvellous experience of playing with others in the school orchestra;
steel bands, folk-groups, pop-groups and combinations of these;
listening to music of all kinds – the diversity is important because many children are constantly surrounded by pop music and need to hear other kinds as well.

...rama

...ildren at this stage are often quite ...inhibited about drama and some

delightful productions emerge, especially if drama, art, music and creative writing are all combined. Your children may experience:

- free acting and miming, with the theme chosen either by the children or the teacher;
- the set play, which when imaginatively produced can achieve such good results that you will feel your children have gained immeasurably from this exciting experience;
- productions arranged by the staff, often with the words, music and sound effects composed and played by the children and the scenery and costumes made in the craft sessions;
- choral speech, verse-speaking and poetry lend themselves to work with a large class of children of mixed abilities. Shy children can often be persuaded to participate with the others. Drama and its assocated

activities provide plenty of opportunity for individual children to shine. The whole experience of drama – with the costumes, scenery, make-up, lighting, music, stage, curtains and the rehearsals leading to the great day of the performance in front of an audience – is magical and no child should miss it.

Physical education

The aims

This is a time of quick physical growth and abundant energy. Hand and eye co-ordination has improved and children are beginning to discover how to use the control they have gained in physical movement and to delight in perfecting their achievements. They have acquired more stamina and self-confidence. Physical maturation, with its changes and subsequent problems, is not yet upon them and they often possess a lithe and graceful physique, capable of marvellous agility.

The physical education lesson. Children work to their own ability, and there is plenty of opportunity for extension and daring.

The PE lesson

Special apparatus is used to extend the children's physical activities. This will be more demanding than at infant level but will continue to include many of the same type of activities. Detailed instruction is often given, in preparation for new movements and a more polished performance is expected. The lesson is likely to be more structured at this stage.

Games

The skills required for football, netball, rounders, tennis, cricket and other games are practised and extended and when the time is right, an introduction may be made to these games. Children must first learn to play as a team, using other team-members to achieve the desired end. This is very hard for many children, who really want to keep the ball to themselves. They may work in

small teams to learn this, and to practise particular skill, e.g. kicking and passing, dodging, hitting the ball, aiming and throwing, catching, or running to a post. They have to learn to take turns and sha the excitement. Team games are often played as a lead into the traditional game Here, childen can learn to accept the rule respect the umpire and how to cope witl success and defeat. At the upper end of school, teams may be chosen to represer the school in these traditional games anc matches may be played against other schools. Some schools prefer to leave all t competitive activity for later and concentrate instead on the basic skills.

Swimming

This takes its place in the school curriculu Certificates are often awarded for achievement, starting with the first few triumphant strokes, right up to the advanced stage of life-saving.

These help to spur the children on to greater efforts and provide a visible reward.

Dancing

There are many variations in this area and I hope your children will experience at least some of them. In your school, you may find modern dancing, folk-dancing, free movement to music or the occasional disco. Folk-dancing has experienced something of a revival recently; it is eminently suitable for both boys and girls of this age, being very energetic and simple – the patterns of movement are repetitive.

Extra activities

Some schools follow the British Amateur Gymnastic Association (BAGA) programmes as an after-school activity. The teacher responsible invites those children to join who are ready to participate. The results of this work are some really beautiful movements, performed with daring, control and elegant finish. Certificates are awarded at the various stages and displays are sometimes given for parents.

Other occasional activities may include cross-country running, orienteering (this is following a set course, using directions and compass), sports days, swimming galas and sponsored walks.

Clothing for PE

The same practices apply at junior level as in the infant/first school. Sometimes at this age children change into special PE shorts and T-shirts. Outside games such as netball and football require suitable shoes. Please continue to mark all clothing and equipment clearly.

If special clothing for PE is required by your school and you have any financial difficulty over this, there are ways of helping, so do mention this to your Headteacher, who will tell you what to do.

Religious education

Some thorny questions

The teaching of religion always arouses great controversy. Many problems arise:

- The majority of people in this country now only follow the Christian faith nominally. Should we, then, continue to present Christianity to our children as being the religion of the people of this country?
- What about schools (and there are quite a number) where the religion of the majority of the pupils is not Christianity? Should we continue to promote it, even though this may upset many parents and children?
- Should we discuss all the major religions in the hope of reducing prejudice and promoting more tolerance and understanding?
- Should we concentrate on teaching ethics – codes of behaviour – and show how the various religions support these?
- Should we abandon the teaching of religion altogether in our schools and leave it all to parents at home? Would this mean that many children never meet it at all?

You see what a thorny question it is; so you will understand the dilemma many Headteachers find themselves in when thinking about how to present religion in their schools. Most Headteachers believe that their parents want this teaching to continue. They do their best to interpret the 1944 Education Act in a way which suits their children.

The assembly

The assembly itself is likely to be run on similar lines to the infant/first school assembly. There may be visitors from outside to talk about an aspect of their work – the supervisor of the local old people's home or the Oxfam organiser, for example. Traditional and modern hymns may be sung and readings may be taken from the Bible, as well as other sources.

Materialism all around us

Religious education (no matter from which creed) is important for all children bcause it concentrates on the spiritual aspects of life, instead of the material. Materialism is evident all around us – street advertisements, television commercials, general life from day to day – all thinking about what to eat, what to wear, what to buy, how to improve your house, your appearance. No wonder our children grow up thinking that these are the only things that matter. The focus in RE is on other things; thoughts about God; what sort of people we are; other people's feelings; how we can know what is right; what is really important and what doesn't matter. Junior and middle school children are not too young to start thinking about these matters. They often demonstrate this by asking the most profound questions.

Helping at home

Reading

To encourage reading at home:

1 Continue reading to your children and reading with them. For a short period you should do this daily – to establish the habit and to provide the constant practice required. Take turns, reading a paragraph each. Discuss the book to make sure your child has understood.
2 Ask the teacher to lend you some suitable books for the children to read at home or games to play (to fix the sounds or memorise irregular words).
3 Try to establish a 'reading environment' at home. Let the children see you enjoying a book or newspaper; let them look up recipes, addresses or football

results. For reluctant readers, set a particular time when you all read. You can compare notes on your books.
4 Generally, boys are less interested in reading than girls. When boys do read they seem to prefer factual books to fiction. Reference books, sports record timetables and atlases are all useful to encourage the reading habit. If they ha a hobby, find books which relate to th and the motivation to read will be ther Books of jokes and comics are good starters with boys.

The Centre for the Teaching of Reading (see address list) issues a useful list of boc for reluctant readers entitled What Can I Read?

Oral work

You can help to encourage confident speech in your children:

- by expecting proper answers to your questions – don't let them get away with a mumbled reply or a shrug;
- by starting discussions on a wide varie of subjects on a serious level. Hold conversation at meal-times, in the car when shopping;
- by playing word games, such as word associations, rhyming words, opposite etc;
- by teaching your children formal greetings which will help them to brea the ice.

Spelling

You can help at home with spelling in a number of ways:

1 If your children come home with a list spellings, work with them in the learni of these words and be sure to test the
2 Make sure they can use a dictionary.
   a) Check that they know the order of the alphabet by heart. If not, write out for them and help them to lear it.

b) Ask them to find a section of the dictionary by letter. Think of the letters as 'near the beginning', 'in the middle' or 'near the end' – providing a clue where to look.

c) Using a few words beginning with the same letter (e.g. doll, drum and desk), show them how to look at the second letter in each word to find them in the dictionary.

d) Then embark on looking at the third letter, and so on.

3 You can buy simple crossword puzzle books and general word puzzle-books. These are good value, especially on a long journey.

Mathematics

1 Children should know the tables by about the age of 8 or 9. If yours find these difficult to remember, make a table game.

Remember that tables only need go to 10 now that we work in a system of tens.

Play 'Snap' with a similar set of cards. You will need to repeat the possibilities to make the game fun.

$$4 \times 6 = \qquad 8 \times 3 = \qquad 2 \times 12 =$$

or

$$3 \times 4 = \qquad 6 \times 2 = \qquad 12 \times 1 =$$

2 Continue the 'maths with everything' approach as recommended for the infant school; now, though, it will become more complicated and therefore more interesting. For instance, get out the map, notice scale, find distances, work out speeds and times of journeys. Calculate the cost and amount of the petrol; find out how much it is costing each person, and so on.

3 Play any mathematical games you can get hold of, such as Round Europe, involving calculating distances from the capitals.

4 Make sure the children do any homework set. Check that they take their work back to school.

5 During holidays, children often enjoy working in a 'fun' maths book.

6 Much of what the children are learning may be new to you, especially at the upper end of the school. How would you like to learn along with the children? The school would be delighted to lend you a book and give any help you needed. Evening meetings at school will help and maths courses for parents are available at evening classes.

Science

Encourage your children's interest in science. You won't have to do much because this is a natural activity for children – collecting, examining, weighing, testing, experimenting – all children do this, given a suitable environment.

Practical work in maths continues to be important in the Junior School.

Some practical suggestions

Working with sand:

1 How long does it take for sand to trickle through a flower-pot? Compare different rates with different pots. Time them by counting, or with a stop-watch.
2 How much weight is needed to make a sand-castle collapse? Place a light plastic lid on top and add small weights one by one; use small stones or beans or safety-pins for weights.
3 How much does sand weigh? Does wet sand weigh more than dry sand?

Working with paper:

1 Have a tug-of-war with various kinds of paper – which kind is the strongest? Try newspaper, tissue-paper, drawing paper, etc.
2 Can paper float? Try out several kinds and see which floats the longest.

3 How far can you throw a piece of pape Does it go further if you screw it up? (fold it in a special way?

Children enjoy bits of special science equipment:

● magnets of various types, with bits an pieces to test – pins, nails, paper-clips, foil, etc;
● a magnifying glass;
● a compass, for finding directions;
● a torch battery, a bulb and a bulb-holc and some wire, to set up a circuit and make the light glow.

Project work

You can help by channelling your childre interests towards history and geography and make them aware that it is all arounc them. Notice the various styles of architecture, often showing all the differe periods in history. Visit your local museum to look at old-fashioned costume, transport or home interiors. Encourage older relatives to talk about their childhood, schooling and life-style.

Look at maps with the chidren, both of your immediate locality and also of the world. They enjoy finding countries, rivers and towns. Perhaps you have some objects which come from abroad? Link these up with their places of origin and try to discover how they came to you. On radio and television we hear about a football match in Mexico, a cross-Atlantic race, a student protest in Beijing, a freeze-up in Siberia – where are all these places? What is it like there? Use the travel and history programmes as a basis for discussion. Borrow books from your library to find out more. Collect pictures of a special country and make a scrap-book with captions – there's so much to be done!

Creative work

The first thing you can do is to make sure that you give all creative activities their proper value and encourage your children in their efforts. You won't have to pressurise your children into these activities at home once they have learnt the techniques – they are so inventive. A treasure chest similar to the one suggested for younger children is really all that is required. Adapt this to suit their improved skills. Children of this age are not usually satisfied with bodged-up results; they like the results to look good and will spend some time attaining this.

For drama at home, you need a dressing-up box. You can promise to lend some make-up when the show is fit for an audience. You do need a group of children for successful drama so perhaps the acting session could be combined with a social occasion.

Music

Music at home requires a little more

supervision. If your children are learning to play the recorder or any other instrument, it is absolutely essential that they practise it, however painful the initial sounds may be. See that they do a little every day; this is better than leaving all the practice until the day before the lesson then trying to cram it all into one session. Do your best to encourage them, because it really is difficult to master any musical instrument and the end result is very rewarding.

Listening to music is something you can encourage at home, too. What about letting the children choose a record or tape for you all to enjoy over a meal? Children respond to strong tunes and rhythms, as well as music which evokes a mood. Try some Strauss waltzes, some brisk marches, Greek folk songs and dances. Let them hear different instruments – trumpet, cello, the evocative pan-pipes, the harpischord, and so on.

You can often borrow records and tapes from your local library, to widen your choice. What if they always choose pop music? Well, I would be hard-hearted, and limit their choice, 'Today, it's this or that, which would you like?' They should realise that music does not only consist of pop, even if they return to it in the end.

Listening to live music, is a different experience from hearing it recorded; it has so much more impact; you may be able to find a local concert, or a band playing outside, or even school performances are a good introduction to different kinds of music.

Physical education

Check that your children actually take their PE and games equipment to school on the days they need them. Children tend to be slightly scatter-brained, and can experience awful traumas when they find they have forgotten their gear. Eventually, of course, they must learn to organise themselves but, at first, a little supervision is supportive.

If your children are keen games players,

89

it may be possible for you to arrange some special holiday tuition or practice for them. The National Playing Fields Association (see address list) can probably help link you up with a centre near you.

Religious education

If you hold firm religious views, you will already have made a start on your children's religious education. However, it is much more difficult for those who hold no definate beliefs, or who strongly avoid these; so what should be done?

1 Don't be shy about discussing religious beliefs and practices with your children; these strongly influence the life of nations (and therefore our lives) and we should try to understand what drives others, and ourselves, into such drastic actions.

2 Discuss the rights and wrongs of your daily lives. Should I have done that? How would you like it if . . . ? That sounded awfully rude, did you realise that? It does help children to have a yardstick against which they can measure their own, and other's, behaviour. If right and wrong ways of going on are never mentioned, how can they make decisions?

3 Try to encourage that old-fashioned virtue, integrity, which as far as children are concerned, means:
   • if you say you are going to do something, then do it;
   • be honest – no 'pinching' or 'nicking';
   • be truthful – no fibs or evasions;
   • stick to your convictions, even when these are unpopular;
   • be helpful when you can; be kind rather than callous;
   • be gentle rather than rough, polite rather than rude, and so on.

Try to help them to mature into reliable people, who can be depended upon in daily interactions. This won't come all at once, but it is something to strive for, and you won't go far wrong if you work towards these ends.

The final year

What should our children have achieved the time they are ready to start their secondary education? Generally speaking they will be ready to meet the new challenges, the skills they have acquired i the primary school will help them to face the future with confidence. As well as having acquired some background knowledge of history, geography, science and religious education, most children wi be able to:

• read with fluency and understanding, use reference books and dictionaries; extract information from books;
• express their ideas and feelings in speech, confidently and clearly;
• write in clear sentences, with reasonabl handwriting, spelling and punctuation
• write stories, descriptions, factual accounts, etc. using a wide vocabular
• work successfully in many areas of mathematics, including computation; will know their tables; will be able to u their knowledge in practical situations and for solving abstract problems; wil understand mathematical language ar symbols;
• use a computer and other forms of technology and have experienced wh. these can do;
• have experienced work in science, anc made a start on problem-solving;
• enjoy a variety of creative work and u the relevant tools sensibly;
• enjoy and use the control they have gained in physical movements and be able to work with tenacity; use the games' skills they have developed, an be able to work with a team;
• be able to hold their own in a larger community, and to contribute usefully to it.

You have always to bear in mind that children mature at different rates and ha different abilities, so they will certainly n

Self-contained and happy children at play.

all have reached this stage in every respect. By the end of the junior school, their inherent strengths and weaknesses begin to show up; it is rare for children to be good at everything.

Middle schools, which keep their children up to the age of 12 or 13 will expect their pupils to achieve much more:

all basic difficulties in the skills sorted out;
more work with computers and other forms of technology;
further extension in maths, and particularly in science;
art, craft, music and drama becoming more demanding and sophisticated;
subject teaching firmly established;
the introduction of a second language;

- more opportunity to help run the school themselves;
- more responsibility for their own work and behaviour;
- and more homework.

The strength of our Primary Schools probably lies in the emphasis on the development of the whole child – personality, self-confidence and maturity, as well as the physical, creative and academic education.

During these years, the precious qualities of intellectual curiosity, imagination and abundant energy are stimulated and harnessed to educational ends. You will feel proud of your confident children and proud, too, of the part you have played in helping to educate them.

The Glossary

Ability grouping within a mixed ability class, children of similar abilities may be grouped together for teaching purposes.

Activity method one which is based on the fact that children learn most effectively from the practical experience of doing things themselves.

Ancillary staff help teachers in schools, with tasks other than teaching. Welfare assistants in primary schools and Laboratory assistants in secondary schools come under this heading.

Assisted places scheme government financial help, on a sliding scale, offered to bright pupils for attendance in independent schools. Entry is by examination. Details may be obtained from the DES (Department of Education and Science) or direct from those schools which participate in the scheme.

Autistic children suffer from a mental condition which makes all relationships difficult. Symptoms may be an apparent inability to talk, aloofness and extreme restraint. It is often diagnosed early and children can be educated to a high standard.

Basic skills usually refers to the three Rs – reading, writing and arithmetic.

Catchment area area designated by the local authority around the school, which gives children living within it an automatic right of entry into that school. In a popular school, children living outside the catchment area may not be admitted to it.

Child guidance clinic centre where psychologists offer advice and treatment to families and their children, who have been referred to them by schools, family doctors or by the parents themselves. All local authorities provide this service.

Computation in mathematics, this means calculations with numbers, reckoning.

Concept means the general idea behind the work. Children often appear to understand a piece of work, but have not really grasped the concept. For example, a child may be able to say that area is 'length by breadth', but not understand that area relates to surface measurement and is measured in the most convenient unit of squares. The concept has not been understood, though the words have been repeated.

Educational priority area area of social deprivation, usually in inner cities or very remote rural areas, which requires extra financial support for education.

Educational psychologist specialises in child psychology and is available for consultation by parent and schools. Children with emotional, behavioural or learning difficulties are assessed and helped.

Educational welfare officer local authority worker, responsible for the welfare of children. He or she dea with such matters as regular attendance, punctuality, children in difficulties, either at home or at school. Educational welfare officers visit families and provide useful link between home and school.

Exclusion from school children can be excluded from school, if they have an infectious or contageous disease, or headlice.

Expulsion the refusal of a school to allow a child to attend usually because of severe behavioural problem which disrupt the normal school routine. This is very rare in primary schools. This action must be confirmed by the school governors, and parents have the right to appeal to the local education authority.

Free school set up by parents and others, to provide an alternative to the state system. They are not fee-paying and are often used by children who have opted out of the normal school system altogether. Sometimes, after a period in one of these schools, the will agree to return to the normal school.

In care children are placed 'in care' if circumstances force the local authority to assume parental rights ov them. They may be in moral or physical danger, or o of control of their parents. Such children are placed in community home or a foster home.

Intelligence test claims to measure the ability to reason verbally or non-verbally (with or without words). Formerly, these were part of the 11+ exam, but now they are used as an indication only for any child's ability.

Integration/integrated day occurs where the day is not timetabled for all subjects, but each is included a the opportunity arises. The basic skills are not norma taught in this way, but further practice is provided in them in the integrated work, which usually includes history, geography, science etc. Project work often integrates all areas of the curriculum.

Irregular words are those which cannot be sounded out using phonetics. Children have to learn to recognise them visually or by association.

Language development general term for learning to talk, use words, form sentences, and acquire a wide vocabulary. It is a vital part of the process of learning at school in all areas, but especially in reading and writing.

Literacy is the ability to read and write.

Multi-racial education takes into account the cultural and religious background of other ethnic groups in the community. Most local authorities provide language classes for those whose first language is not English. In primary schools, an effort is made to ensure that all children have some understanding of the cultures of other races.

Numeracy is the ability to work with numbers. To be innumerate, is to be unable to do this.

Open-plan schools traditional classrooms are exchanged for open learning areas, where all the necessary books and equipment for that subject are stored. These areas are used by all the children, either in turn or as they need them. There may be a maths area, a music area, a book corner, a science bay, an art and craft area, and so on. Each teacher will have the overall responsibility for a class of children, and a home base, for class teaching and discussions. But when working, the children will move to the area most suited to their work.

Peripatetic teacher specialist who travels from school to school, to give lessons, e.g. in music or drama or remedial reading.

Reading age derived from tests which compare children's reading ability against the average ability for their age. Those with a reading age lower than their actual age, will need extra help. Most primary school children have a reading age above their actual age, and some significantly so.

Reception class first class in the infant/first school.

Record card most schools keep a record card showing children's progress, as they move through the school. Some local authorities provide a standard form of record-card for all their schools. The record contains the family details taken by the Head on admission, all test results, examples of work, copies of annual reports, and so on. Records are usually passed on to the next school the child attends. There is a move to make it possible for parents to see these records and many Heads will do so on request. The records should not contain subjective, personal comments by any staff member, which might prejudice the child's future.

Remedial teacher specialises in teaching children with learning difficulties; often found in primary schools and, where there is a need, in secondary schools.

Rising-fives refers to children who reach their fifth birthday, during their first term at school. Some local education authorities admit the rising-fives, others wait until the term following the fifth birthday, strictly according to the law.

Rote learning by rote means learning by heart. Formerly, most teaching was based on this. It is used now for learning tables, alphabet and similar useful things, but always after the understanding has been acquired.

School phobia extreme fear of going to school. (Not to be confused with a quite normal reluctance most children show at times.) This is a psychological condition and needs professional help.

Setting withdrawal of children of a similar ability group from a class of mixed ability, for the purpose of better teaching, in a particular subject. It is commonly in use in comprehensive schools and in some middle and primary schools.

Social services department is the local government department in charge of children in need. It is responsible for grants to play groups, for day nurseries, arranges holidays for needy children. It employs social workers to help families under stress, to identify children in moral or physical danger, and to take responsibility for children in care.

Speech therapy is the treatment given by the speech therapist, who is a specialist dealing in speech disorders. Treatment may be suggested by the parents, the school doctor, or a teacher, and will take place at a clinic.

Streaming occurs where children are placed in classes according to their academic ability. This practice is seen in many independent schools but most comprehensives prefer setting to streaming, as being equally efficient for teaching purposes, but less devisive.

Team-teaching occurs when a group of teachers take joint responsibility for several classes of children. Each teacher will concentrate on the area of the curriculum which is his or her strongest, so that all children will benefit from this. This system is often used in open-plan schools and in some middle schools.

Truancy means absence from school for reasons other than the accepted ones – illness, family holidays (up to a fortnight) or a crisis in the home. It is usually initiated by the children themselves. Any suspected truancy is reported to parents at once.

Visual discrimination means visually spotting differences in appearance, shape, colour, size, position, between various objects, letters, sequences, etc. This quality of sharp observation is greatly in use when learning to read and spell, and in much maths work.

An address list

The Advisory Centre for Education runs an Advisory Service, offering specific advice for difficulties, especially those connected with learning. It puts parents in touch with others in their area.
32 Trumpington Street, Cambridge, CB2 1QY

Anything Left-Handed Ltd sells a variety of equipment for left-handed people. It will supply schools.
65 Baker Street, London W1

The British Association for Early Childhood Education gives information about education for the under-fives.
Montgomery Hall, Kennington Oval, London SE11 5SW

British Dyslexia Association
Church Lane, Pappard, Oxon RG9 5JN

British Broadcasting Corporation (BBC) for all schools' programmes. They will send you a complete timetable of programmes on request.
35 Marylebone High Street, London W1M 4AA

Campaign for the Advancement of State Education (CASE). A pressure group of parents, teachers and others, who are concerned to keep the standard of state education high. It has national officers and local branches.
25 Leyborne Park, Kew Gardens, Richmond, Surrey.

Centre for the Teaching of Reading. This centre provides guidance and advice to teachers and parents, on the teaching of reading, spelling and linked activities. It publishes many excellent pamphlets at a very reasonable cost.
University of Reading School of Education, 29 Eastern Avenue, Reading, Berkshire.

Child Development Research Unit supplies a free list of toys suited for particular purposes, including those for handicapped children. It supplies names and addresses of manufacturers.
University of Nottingham, University Park, Nottingham, NG7 2RD

Children's Legal Centre. This centre gives advice on the law, in relation to children's rights. It can help parents involved in disputes between schools or local authorities.
20 Compton Terrace, London NL 2UN

Child Poverty Action Group. This voluntary organisation researches into child poverty, can give advice to parents and issues a journal.
1 Macklin Street, London WC2B 5NH

Cruse offers help and relief to widows and their children. Clubs provide social activities and practical support. It issues a newsletter and information sheets.
The Charter House, 6 Lion Gate Gardens, Richmond, Surrey.

Department of Education for Northern Ireland deals with all matters concerning education in the province.
Rathgael House, Ballee Road, Belfast, BT19 2PR.

Department of Education and Science is responsible for general policy-making for schools and colleges in England. It is the final court of appeal for disputes between parents and their local authorities. It can advise and recommend, accept or reject plans for re-organisation in schools. It finances some universities and educational research, and has control over the supply of teachers, and the building of schools and colleges.
Elizabeth House, York Road, London SE1 7PH

Dyslexia Institute. A charitable organisation which gives advice to parents and helps to train teachers to deal with this condition.
133 Gresham Road, Staines, Middlesex, TW18 2JX

The Early Learning Centre provides its customers with a guide to the best toys and books for the under-eights.
11 Crown Street, Reading, RG1 2TQ

Education Otherwise. A group of parents, experienced in home-based education, who give advice to others wishing to educate their own children.
25 Common Lane, Hemmingford Abbots, Cambridgeshire, CE18 9AN

Educational Supply Association (ESA). This publisher issues free catalogues with details of toys, games and educational equipment, stating the age and purpose of these.
Pinnacles, PO Box 22, Harlow CM19 5AY

Galt Early Stages issue a useful catalogue of children's games and toys.
Brookfield House, Cheadle, Cheshire

Gifted Children's Information Centre. Issues publications which give practical help to children of high intelligence.
941 Warwick Road, Solihull, B91 3EX

Gingerbread run social and self-help groups for one-parent families throughout the country. It can offer legal advice.
9 Poland Street, London W1V 3DG

Independent Schools Information Service (ISIS). Provides information to parents about independent schools, their fees and facilities.
56 Buckingham Gate, London SW1E 6AN

Independent Television (ITV) provides a complete timetable of schools' programmes.
Schools' Programmes, ITV, 70 Brompton Road, London SW3

National Association for Gifted Children (NAGC). This registered charity seeks to provide opportunities and extending activities for gifted children, and to encourage their development within the school system. It has local branches.
1 South Audley Street, London W1Y 5DQ

National Association of Governors and Managers (NAGM). Seeks to improve the quality of the contribution made at schools' governors meetings, by arranging conferences, and issuing publications.
81 Rustlings Road, Sheffield, S11 7AB

National Association for Multi-Racial Education (NAME). This voluntary organisation seeks to improve the education of children in multiracial areas, by teacher-training and the provision of special materials in schools.
PO Box 9, Walsall, West Midlands, WS1 3SF

National Association for Remedial Education (NARE) is an association for all people working with remedial education. Organises conferences, issues publications, books to read, games to play etc.
Mrs M Bushell, 4 Old Croft Road, Walton-on-the-Hill, Staffordshire

National Association in Support of Small Schools. This pressure group offers advice to parents whose schools are threatened with closure, because of their size.
91 King Street, Norwich, NR1 1PE

National Campaign for Nursery Education provides pressure to encourage more state nursery education. Campaigns to prevent the closure of threatened nurseries.
3 St. George's Terrace, Coulsden Road, Caterham-on-the-Hill, Surrey, CR3 5NH

National Council for Civil Liberties (NCCL). For any matter connected with children's rights and those of adults.
186 King's Cross Road, London WC1X 9DE

National Council for One-Parent Families. Issues help and advice to one-parent families and single pregnant women. Provides legal and practical help. Publishes booklets.
255 Kentish Town Road, London NW5 2LX

National Council for Special Educaton. An organisation for everyone connected with special education; issues publication, and has local branches.
Wood Street, Stratford-upon-Avon, CV37 6JE

National Federation of City Farms
The Old Vicarage, 66 Fraser Street, Windmill Hill, Bedminster, Bristol, BS3 4LY

National Federation of Parent-Teacher Associations. These associations are organised within schools by parents and teachers, in order to bring the two groups closer together, and to arrange educational, social and fund-raising events.
43 Stonebridge Road, Northfleet, Gravesend, Kent.

National Playing Fields Association. Keeps a register of all adventure playgrounds, including those for handicapped children, arranges holiday play schemes, lists of these are available for each county.
57b Catharine Plane, London SW1

Parents National Educational Union (PNEU) gives guidance to parents who wish to educate their children at home.
Murray House, Vandon Street, London SW1E 0AJ

Pre-School Playgroups Association (PPA). A charity offering advice and help to those wishing to start a playgroup. It organises training to playgroup leaders.
Alford House, Averling Street, London, SE11 5DH

School Curriculum Development Committee (SCDC). The national organisation which studies curriculum development in schools.
Newcombe House, 45 Notting Hill Gate, London W11 3JB

Scottish Education Department (SED). The governmental department in Scotland responsible for Education. It is under the authority of the Secretary of State for Scotland.
New St. Andrew's House, St. James' Gate, Edinbrugh EH1 3SY

Time Out for Kids. Arranges holiday activities for children – trips in and around the city, museums, galleries, sports, etc. in Liverpool. Liverpool Confederation for the Advancement of State Education, Liverpool.

Watch organise clubs for children, to encourage an active part in tracking down and recording pollution.
32 Trumpington Street, Cambridge, CB2 1QY

Welsh Office is responsible for Welsh administration and education.
31 Cathedral Road, Cardiff, CF1 9UJ

Young Ornithologists' Club is the youth branch of the Royal Sciety for the Protection of Birds. It caters for children up to 15 years, and hols meetings, film-shows, courses, projects and outings. It has local branches.
The Lodge, Sandy, Bedfordshire, SG19 2DL

This list shows the national headquarters of the societies, but most of them have regional branches, which you could find out from your local library or from the local branch of the Citizens Advice Burearu. This organisation is very helpful over all matters.

Index